07

Dear
Lucy,

May
Hashem
bless you
with many
miracles!

Warmly,
Yitte

Small
Miracles
for Women

Also available by Yitta Halberstam and Judith Leventhal

Small Miracles from Beyond:
Dreams, Visions and Signs that Link Us to the Other Side

Small
Miracles
for Women

EXTRAORDINARY COINCIDENCES
of HEART *and* SPIRIT

YITTA HALBERSTAM *&*
JUDITH LEVENTHAL

STERLING ETHOS
New York

STERLING ETHOS
New York

An Imprint of Sterling Publishing
1166 Avenue of the Americas
New York, NY 10036

This Sterling Ethos edition published in 2015.

First edition published in 2000 by Adams Media Corporation.

ISBN 978-1-4549-1283-5

Distributed in Canada by Sterling Publishing
^{c}/o Canadian Manda Group, 664 Annette Street
Toronto, Ontario, Canada M6S 2C8
Distributed in the United Kingdom by GMC Distribution Services
Castle Place, 166 High Street, Lewes, East Sussex, England BN7 1XU
Distributed in Australia by Capricorn Link (Australia) Pty. Ltd.
P.O. Box 704, Windsor, NSW 2756, Australia

For information about custom editions, special sales, and premium and corporate
purchases, please contact Sterling Special Sales at 800-805-5489
or specialsales@sterlingpublishing.com.

Manufactured in the United States of America

2 4 6 8 10 9 7 5 3 1

www.sterlingpublishing.com

In loving memory of my mother, Claire Halberstam, a visionary and an original, who was truly authentic to herself, and is still sorely missed today.

~ *Yitta Halberstam*

For my mother, Rose Frankel, and my mother-in-law and aunt of blessed memory, Anne Leventhal and Margaret Handler. Each one an exemplary woman in her own right.

-- *Judith Leventhal*

Contents

PREFACE

*O*ur thanks go first and foremost to YOU, our cherished readers, whose enthusiasm for the message of our books has been boundless and immensely gratifying. Since the first Small Miracles book was published in 1997, we have been both inundated, and enormously moved, by your kind letters, heartened to know that our series has brought you joy and comfort. Your excitement has in turn galvanized *us*, and therefore you are the true co-creators of our books. We applaud YOU for your open hearts and warm response, as well as the hundreds of incredible stories you have sent along our way.

After Sterling Publishing published a new book in the series, *Small Miracles from Beyond* (which came out in Fall 2014), we were thrilled that they also decided to relaunch *Small Miracles for Women*—since women are our biggest supporters and most ardent fans. Small Miracles books have been published in China, Japan, Indonesia, Thailand, France, Brazil, Argentina, Korea, Italy, Greece, Turkey, Hungary, Israel, Germany, and Canada, and worldwide, women are our primary readers. Thank you for creating this global phenomenon!

The overwhelming support of women for our books doesn't really surprise us: Women always seem to be in tune with the messages sent to us through the miracle of coincidences. We know that we tend to live more in our hearts than in our heads, and we filter reality through the prism of spirit. Some would argue that women are more intuitive than men, more open to life's mysteries, more mystically inclined, and we would certainly agree.

Despite our ever-demanding schedules and crazy, harried lives, women especially need to take time to stop and see the magic of the tiniest moments. These are Small Miracles, and we dedicate this book to you.

This collection celebrates the milestones and markers of every woman's life: birth, love, marriage, friendship, and beyond. We have searched the country to find true stories that would speak to women of all ages and of all faiths. Quite simply, *Small Miracles for Women* addresses our shared experiences—the triumphs and the defeats, the celebrations and the losses sustained during a lifetime. And woven throughout these stories is the magic, the sense of awe, the understanding that these experiences are being orchestrated by a loving hand that gently guides and connects us all.

Do women live too deeply? Being conscious, being awake, being open is part of the divine experience, part of feeling integrated into the cosmic order. So we say, you can never live deeply enough! We hope that this book will continue to open doors into that deeper, more profound experience and be a corridor to the mindfulness that makes life that much more sweet. For in a world where chaos and a sense of existential meaninglessness often swirl around us, possessing the knowledge that we are part of a divine plan and have sacred purpose is infinitely comforting.

May we all continue to be blessed with Small Miracles—both large and small—and with the wisdom to recognize them when they touch our lives.

THE HOUSE AT THE END OF THE LANE

*T*he pain hit with sudden fury. No, thought Monica. I can't be having this baby now. Not here in the car!

Frantically, she looked around. The country road was dark and deserted. No house beckoned, no phone booth appeared. Outside, icy winds pounded the car. It was almost midnight, New Year's Eve 1998, and she was all alone. The pain lashed so hard she couldn't hit the brake.

How had it come to this? Only two days ago, her doctor had smiled reassuringly. "Everything looks fine, Monica. The baby should be here mid-February." Confident she wouldn't deliver for six weeks, Monica had decided to make the hour's drive to her parents' house in Maryland and surprise them for New Year's Eve. Now here she was, on the outskirts of her hometown, screaming with terror as she felt the baby coming right in the car.

Just go to the hospital. It's only ten minutes away, she told herself. But it was no use. She could feel the baby about to appear. Oh God, please don't let it come just yet; it's going to suffocate. . . . Please God. . . . Fighting back hysteria, she took off her shoes so she could pull down her pants. She was now near her old high school. As she desperately tried to figure out how to drive and deliver the baby at the same time, she noticed a neighborhood she'd never seen before. She turned into it and found herself on a little cul-de-sac. Somehow, she maneuvered the car to a stop and stumbled out into the freezing night.

Four houses, all with lights on, faced her. Grandma, Monica prayed. You can see from heaven. Help me. Where should I go?

Without thinking, without understanding why, Monica ran past the three houses that were closest. Staggering with excruciating pain, shivering in her stocking feet, feeling the baby coming any second, Monica chose the house that was farthest away.

"Help me!" she screamed, pounding on the door. "I'm having a baby! Call 911!"

No one answered. Don't make me deliver my baby all by myself on this porch, God . . . help me, please . . .

"Don't let her in." A man was speaking on the other side of the door. "There's a crazy lady out there."

Now a woman's voice answered, softly but firmly. "I'm opening the door anyway," she said.

The door swung open. An elderly woman in a bathrobe waved Monica inside. "Don't worry," she said kindly. "My daughter is here."

In the upstairs bedroom of her parents' house, Dianne slept, oblivious to the pandemonium below. That morning in Virginia, the snow had been falling so hard that she had almost decided to cancel her visit to her parents. But by early afternoon, the snow had let up enough for her to risk the four-hour drive to Maryland. The trip had been exhausting, and Dianne had fallen asleep at ten o'clock, too tired to join her parents as they rang in the New Year.

Now her mother's voice roused Dianne from her sleep: "Dianne! Come quick!" And another woman's voice, hysterical: "Oh God help me! My baby's coming!"

Dianne raced out of bed to the top of the stairs. She looked down at the screaming stranger. Then she flew into action. "Mom, call 911! Dad, get sheets!" she barked as she ran down the stairs.

"Everything's going to be okay," she said, taking Monica's hand. "I'm a nurse. I worked labor and delivery for four years. Let's get you upstairs onto a bed."

At the top of the stairs, Monica stopped. "It's coming now!" she screamed. Dianne laid her down and prepared to deliver the baby.

"What position did your last ultrasound show?" Dianne asked.

"Breech. Is it going to be okay?" sobbed Monica.

"Yes, of course. Just try not to push, and keep breathing."

But despite her reassuring words to Monica, Dianne felt sick with panic. The baby was preterm and in breech position. And she had no equipment. How could she possibly deliver this baby alive?

Calm down, Dianne, she told herself. God did not send this woman to you for this baby to die. Just do what you have to do and everything will be fine.

"Monica, I see it coming!" Dianne said. "Don't push!"

At that moment, the doorbell rang and a volunteer emergency worker bounded inside. He was only eighteen years old, nervous and unsure of what to do.

"Get the emergency oxygen and the delivery kit—now!" Dianne ordered. He ran back to the ambulance and returned just as the baby was born into Dianne's waiting hands.

"Congratulations, Monica. You have a boy."

"I don't hear him! Why isn't he crying?" Monica screamed.

Without answering, Dianne unwrapped the cord that was strangling his tiny neck. She suctioned the mucus from his nose with the emergency kit, cut the cord, and stimulated him until he cried.

"Give me oxygen! Quick! He's turning blue!"

As soon as she stabilized his color, Dianne gently placed the baby on Monica.

By now the paramedics had arrived, ready to take Monica to the hospital. "Hold him next to your skin. Your body temperature will help protect him," Dianne said, placing layer upon layer of cloth on top of the baby.

"Good luck!" she called as the paramedics carried Monica and her newborn outside into the fifteen-degree night.

The next day, Dianne walked into Monica's hospital room, carrying flowers. "These are for you," she said, placing them on the windowsill. "And this is for the baby." As she leaned in to hand Monica a teddy bear, she broke into a startled laugh. "Hey! You've got my dad's pillow!"

"How did that happen?" Monica said. "Should I give it back?"

"Keep it. It will bring you luck. "

"You brought me luck, Dianne. Without you . . . my beautiful baby . . . my Jacob . . . would be . . ." Unable to say the word, Monica burst into tears and threw her arms around Dianne's neck. The two women held each other close and cried together.

At last Dianne said, "It wasn't me who brought you luck, Monica. This was meant to be."

"It was a miracle," sobbed Monica.

"There's something I want to ask you," Dianne said. "This morning we went out and locked your car. And we saw where you parked it. There were three houses closer than ours. So why on earth did you choose us?"

"I really don't know. I remember I prayed to my grandmother to help me. And then without thinking, I ran to your house. That doesn't make sense, does it? I was in my stocking feet, and I was in so much pain that your house seemed a hundred miles away. I don't know. I just chose you."

~ Peggy Sarlin

THE PROMISE BRACELET

*T*he glitter of green stones drew me to the display case. The light bounced off silver and glass. Amid the throng of holiday shoppers, I stood in the corner area reserved for fine jewelry and gazed at the bracelet, noticing its unique handiwork. The beaten silver, fashioned to resemble diamond chips, was exquisite, and it was encrusted with dozens of dark green emeralds. I knew this was a one-of-a-kind treasure.

As I admired the intricate piece, I remembered a promise my husband had made. David had bought me a lovely gift on our honeymoon four years earlier. He had selected an emerald-green Austrian crystal and seed-pearl bracelet in honor of my May birthstone. As he fastened it on my wrist, he lovingly said, "I promise you that I will buy you real emeralds someday soon. Just wait." I loved the sentiment of his honeymoon gift, but deep down I excitedly looked forward to the fulfillment of David's promise.

Until that time, however, I still loved wearing my crystal bracelet. I wore it frequently, each time fondly remembering the island boutique where we had found it. Whenever David saw the bracelet, he would smile and reassure me that the time was coming soon when he would keep his promise.

It became our habit over the years to look in every jewelry store window. David's pursuit became symbolic of his devotion to me, and I loved him for it. We wandered in and out of countless shops, becoming somewhat discouraged when we realized that the cost of his promise was well beyond our means. I started to doubt that I would ever own what David desired to give me. David, however, never lost his faith.

On the day I found this particular bracelet, we were in the mall during the last week before Christmas to buy gifts for our children. Finances were tight, and we had agreed there would be no exchange of gifts between us. We had just completed one of the most stressful years of our marriage. With David's diagnosis of Huntington's disease, our lives had forever changed. This fatal neurological disorder had pitched us into a panic, not to mention near bankruptcy.

I looked up into David's eyes and saw love shining even brighter than the green stones. I could tell what was in his mind. Nothing short of this bracelet would satisfy his original honeymoon promise. But I knew there was no way we could possibly afford it. I tried to tell him, but the words died on my lips. He'd had so many disappointments that year; I didn't have the heart to tell him that we absolutely shouldn't consider it.

Thinking fast, I came up with a reason to refuse the offer I knew I couldn't accept. I have large wrists, and normally bracelets don't fit. As the store clerk reverently lifted the object out of the case, I knew it would be too small. The silver and green made a colorful contrast against my brown skin. I silently acknowledged how much I wanted the bracelet while still hoping it would not fit. As the clerk reached around my wrist and closed the intricate clasp, my heart both leaped and then quickly plummeted. It fit! It was perfect. Yet I knew it would be wrong to buy it. The unpaid bills, with more looming in the future, had placed a vise around our checkbook.

I glanced at my husband, my best friend, and saw him beam. This gentle man was now the victim of a very cruel disease. His was a sentence with only one verdict: untimely, slow, and cruel death. My eyes brimmed with tears as I realized we would not live out our dream of growing old together. The jewelry before me was meaningless compared with the hope of living a lifetime with this man. But to David, the bracelet on my wrist would not be just one more bauble in a crowded jewelry box. Rather, this was his love for me displayed for all the world to see. To David, a promise made was a promise to be kept. I sadly realized that he might not have many more months or years in which to keep his promise. Suddenly it became the most important covenant ever made, and I knew that somehow I had to juggle the bills to let him have the honor of keeping it.

"Do you like it?" he whispered. Hearing the hope in his voice, mingled with the adoration in his eyes, was heart-wrenching. It was clear that David cherished me. All he had ever wanted, from the day we met, was to make me happy. I was a lucky woman, indeed.

I heard myself saying, "Yes, honey, I love it. It's exactly what I want."

The clerk reached out to remove the bracelet. I could not believe this little object had worked its way into my heart so quickly.

"How much is it?" I finally asked.

Slowly the man turned over the little white tag.

Two hundred and fifty dollars. Surely this was a mistake!

I had seen enough fine jewelry to know that price was only a fraction of its worth.

The man began to extol the beauty of the item, pointing out the 180 emeralds in a handmade Brazilian setting. But even though $250 was an incredible value, it might as well have been $2,500, given our meager budget.

Without thinking, I asked, "Would you take $225, tax included?" I was amazed to hear myself ask the question, because shops in malls do not normally bargain.

The clerk looked at me in surprise but answered, "That will be fine." Before he could change his mind, I whipped out my credit card, watching David beam with pride. The man quickly handled the transaction, and we were on our way. Every few steps we would stop and look at the bracelet. Before we reached the car, David said, "When I get sicker and eventually am no longer with you, I hope you'll look at each emerald on the bracelet. Every one will remind you of something special we've done: a trip we took, a movie we saw together, or a moment we shared. This will be your memory bracelet."

I began to cry. David's concern was not for his own failing health but for my welfare after he was gone.

As we worked our way home in rush-hour Honolulu traffic, I wondered just how we would pay for the bracelet. Oddly enough, however, I never really panicked. I was somehow only curious about how it would all work out. We talked as we drove, and every so often we looked admiringly at the miracle of the promise kept.

Upon arriving home, I grabbed the mail and began to open it as we walked inside. Among the usual bills were two cards. One was from a church where I had sung several times that year. It was a thank-you note for my music ministry, along with a gift—a check for $200. I was speechless. I reached for the second card and slit it open. Out fell two bills: a twenty and a five. My benefactor preferred to remain anonymous. The card was simply signed, "Anonymous."

I looked up at David, and we both shook our heads in amazement and then began to laugh. Even as I had inexplicably felt the urge to negotiate our price in the mall, the payment of David's promise was already in our mailbox. God had already taken care of every detail, right down to the penny.

The bracelet is just a piece of jewelry, something I could have lived without. But the memories represented by each emerald have helped make me the person I am today.

The exquisite joy of our relationship and the unspeakable grief of dealing with David's disease have allowed me to develop in ways I never could have anticipated. I have thought about God's promise to each of us—that he will be with us every step of the way in life, if we will just ask him.

Just as God has never stopped believing in me, David never stopped believing in his bracelet promise. Each time I wear my emeralds, I count the memories tucked away in my heart, and I feel new courage as I think about David's faith and God's promises.

~ *Carmen Leal-Pock*

SOUL MATES

She was only nineteen years old, but she was wise beyond her years. And she knew enough about life to know that the love she had found at such a young age was pure, good, and enduring.

We are soul mates, she often thought, kindred spirits. How blessed I am to have Ezra* in my life and for such a long time, too.

Their respective mothers—who were good friends—often laughed that their children were destined-to-be from the time they were toddlers. When the women had first met in Warsaw, the two little ones on their laps had made funny faces at each other and then shared a lollipop. Afterwards, they cried as they parted.

Ezra and Miriam went to school together, and their friendship blossomed into love. In high school, they were already a pair. Their mothers rejoiced to see the melding of their families this way but privately wondered if young love could last. It did.

Ezra presented Miriam with a tiny diamond engagement ring on her nineteenth birthday. "I will always love you," he said.

"You are my destined one," she replied.

But destiny had other things in store for them. Hitler's soldiers marched into Warsaw one day, and life as they had known it ceased to exist.

* The names in this story, a dramatization, are pseudonyms.

Miriam caught a glimpse of Ezra at the train station, where the Jews of her neighborhood were being herded into cattle cars. For resettlement they were told. Chaos reigned as crowds jostled, children wailed, soldiers barked orders, mothers cried. But when Miriam saw Ezra boarding one of the cars at the other end of the platform, her heart lurched and time stood still.

"Ezra!" she screamed. "Ezra!"

She dropped her bags and dashed across the platform.

"Miriam!" her mother cried in alarm. "Don't leave me, please!"

"Where do you think you're going?" a soldier said as he blocked her path. "Get back to your line!"

"Please," she begged him. "My fiancé . . . I just saw him . . . I need to talk to him . . . please . . . just for a minute . . ."

"Get back in line," the Nazi hissed. "Now!"

The "resettlement" story was, of course, a lie. The train delivered them to Auschwitz, where Miriam's mother was selected for the gas chambers. Young and still healthy, Miriam was allowed to live, though barely.

Not a day passed that she didn't look for Ezra. When she passed the men's barracks, when a detail of men passed her, she always inspected their ranks yearningly. Her eyes roved ceaselessly. All she asked for was a glimpse of his face. But she didn't know if he was interned at Auschwitz. She didn't even know if he was alive.

She kept on asking everyone she encountered whether they had seen Ezra in Auschwitz or had met him in any of the other camps they had been transferred from, but no one had any news. She refused to believe that he was dead. In her prayers, she begged God to keep him safe. Take me instead of him, she cried.

At the war's end, Auschwitz was liberated, and Miriam was among the skeletal survivors. Her compatriots, after slowly recovering in DP (displaced persons) camps, made their way to new homes in Israel, America, Canada, South America, Australia—but not Miriam. She stayed behind in Europe for more than three years to hunt for Ezra. But he had vanished, and people told her that after three years it was time to give up. "You have to begin life anew," they urged. "Just like us."

How can I live life without Ezra? she wondered. Life has no meaning without him.

There were those who felt compassionate toward her, and those who felt impatient. "Time to move on,'" they exhorted. "Most people never have that kind of love in their life to begin with. Be grateful you had it at all, even if it was just for a brief time."

Finally, Miriam began to feel the futility of her quest. In a DP camp in Sweden, she met Saul, a kind, gentle man with whom she could make a life. She didn't love him; but she liked him well enough. She was honest about her feelings, and he accepted the limitations. Many survivors didn't want to wait for love; they wanted to rebuild their shattered lives as quickly as possible. Camaraderie and companionship were sufficient for them. Their needs were humble; they didn't ask for more.

So they married in Sweden but made plans to emigrate soon. Miriam's entire family had been wiped out, so she felt unattached to any particular place. She assumed, however, that, like most survivors, they would move to Israel or to the United States. When her husband told her he had an excellent opportunity in Port Elizabeth, South Africa, she was taken aback.

"Port Elizabeth?" she asked in dismay. "I never heard of it. Why do you want to go there?"

"A friend of mine—someone who lived in my town before the war—has moved there and established a thriving business. He needs help and would welcome me into his company as a partner. I don't have such an opportunity anywhere else."

"But . . . I thought we would move to a large Jewish community . . . in the United States . . . in Canada. Even Johannesburg would be better. What kind of place is Port Elizabeth?"

"It's a small coastal city, and it does have only a tiny Jewish population," her husband conceded. "But it's the place where I've been offered an opportunity."

Miriam was reluctant and unhappy. She had had visions of relocating to a vibrant, heavily populated Jewish city where the sheer numbers of coreligionists would make rebuilding easier. She was not so sure what kind of life she could make in Port Elizabeth. She felt like a leaf blown off a tree, driven hither and thither, with no control over its destiny.

"So we'll go to Port Elizabeth," she finally shrugged in resignation. "After everything we've been through, what difference does it make?"

It was at a Jewish agency in Port Elizabeth, where she had gone to fill out some papers for German reparations, that she first saw him.

He was bent low over the clipboard, scribbling furiously, but she recognized the nape of his neck, the contour of his head, the color of his hair. She swore she could smell him across the reception room; she inhaled it as one would an aromatic scent.

"Ezra!" she screamed. "Ezra!"

He looked at her, and their eyes locked. His face turned white.

"Miriam! My God, Miriam! You are alive?! Oh, my God, I was told that you were dead!"

"Me, too. I heard you were dead. I hunted for you for three years," she cried.

"I searched for you for two," he said. Then he dropped his eyes to the floor.

"Miriam," he said anguished, "there are things I would say to you, would like to say, but cannot anymore. . . . Miriam, I am married."

"Ezra," she said softly, "you don't have to explain anything to me. I understand . . . you thought I was dead; I was in the same position. I am married, also."

He looked at her sadly. "Miriam . . . what shall we do? It's not as if we are in London or Sydney or even Johannesburg. The Jewish community in Port Elizabeth is very small; our paths will cross often."

"Ezra, we must do the honorable thing. We cannot hurt or humiliate our spouses in any way. I don't think we should tell them about our encounter today, nor the history of our involvement. Why inflict unnecessary pain on them? It would probably cause them tremendous discomfort to know about our past and to know we were living in this same city together. . . . And," she went on with greater conviction, "we must not speak to each other ever again; we cannot. It would be too painful for us, and dangerous."

"But Miriam!" he protested. "Not to talk to you . . . ever! That's too harsh; it's crazy; it's unacceptable."

"Ezra," she said firmly, "I love you very much. I will never love anyone as I love you. But this is what we must do in order to protect the sanctity of our marriages."

For forty years, they lived in the same community in Port Elizabeth—bearing children, raising families, marking milestones—without acknowledging one another's presence ever again. They honored their vows, protected their spouses' dignity, and tried to live life as fully as they could, knowing that the love of their life was leading a parallel existence only a few short blocks away.

Every now and then, in the synagogue, at a wedding, in the local food market, they would encounter one another briefly, and their eyes would flicker longingly at each other. A quick, imperceptible nod was the only greeting that acknowledged the encounter. A dewy, misty look would always appear in Miriam's eyes after one of these encounters, and her heart would ache. She never shared her pain with anyone, and the two would have gone to their graves with the secret, had an extraordinary turn of events not taken place.

After forty years of marriage, Miriam's husband Saul died suddenly one day of a heart attack. And just two months after Saul's death, Ezra's wife was felled by a fatal stroke.

For a full year after their respective spouses' deaths, the two made no attempt to contact each other. But each had heard the news about the other.

They mourned their spouses, with whom they had fashioned good and decent lives, and their grief was deep and sincere. But as they marked the year of mourning, they also listened for news of one another.

After the first *yahrzeit* (anniversary of death) of each spouse had been commemorated, Ezra picked up the phone.

"Miriam?" he said.

At their wedding a few weeks later, Miriam and Ezra finally revealed to their children and close friends the secret they had kept for so many years. They explained how torturous it had been to live in such a small community and see each other constantly, how wrenching it had been—a trial from God. All this time they had never stopped loving each other, but their commitment to their spouses had never wavered either. Forty years later, they were finally able to fulfill the love that the war had aborted.

~ *Yitta Halberstam*

THE MEETING

*S*he had avoided this moment for years, knowing that once she spoke those magic words her life would never be the same. Now the moment was here. Slowly she rose to her feet, her chair loudly scraping against the basement floor. Thirty faces turned to look at her. She took a deep breath and dared herself to plunge ahead. "My name is Ella,* and I'm an alcoholic," she said.

The knowing sympathy she saw in other people's eyes gave her the courage to continue. "I've got to stop drinking. Because it's not just me I'm hurting anymore. I've got a baby now. My Henry . . ." She stopped, overcome by a sudden vision of Henry, smiling and reaching out his chubby little hands to her. "He . . . he's . . . so beautiful. . . . I would die rather than hurt him. Because I know what it's like to be hurt. My father was a drunk, and I'll do anything to keep Henry from feeling the pain that my father caused me."

After the meeting, Ella sat quietly, slumped over in despair. She would never be able to get sober. And even if by some miracle she did, how could she possibly stay sober, day after day, year after year? The meeting had been filled with stories of terrifying struggles, of constant temptations, tragic losses, and hard-fought victories rendered hollow by sudden, sickening falls from grace. The battle for sobriety never ended, no matter

* The names in this story, a dramatization, are pseudonyms.

how safe you thought you were. Even with her love for Henry to guide her, how could she win?

"Ella?" She looked up. A pleasant-looking young woman put her hand on her shoulder and gave it a gentle squeeze. "Don't worry. I can tell you're in it for the long haul."

The long haul . . . many times over the next two years, those words echoed in Ella's mind. Faithfully every day, sometimes twice a day, she attended a support group meeting, gradually finding the strength to give up drink. Sometimes at a meeting she would see Laurie, the pleasant-looking woman, who was battling a deeply ingrained drinking habit. According to the group's rules, everyone kept personal details to a minimum and didn't socialize outside of meetings. But even within these restrictions, Ella began to think of Laurie as her friend. She had such an uncanny knack of saying to Ella exactly what she needed to hear, of finding the perfect words to give her comfort and confidence.

Once, when Ella was panicking about getting through the night, Laurie had nodded gravely. "For you, Ella, it's eighteen minutes at a time." Eighteen minutes at a time! She could probably handle that. And if she could get through eighteen minutes, followed by another eighteen and another, maybe she could get through the long haul after all.

Another time, Ella talked about her father and the rage she felt toward him. She described how he drank away his frustrations as a painter, his mood growing blacker and more dangerous with every sip. Laurie responded by speaking movingly about her own creative struggles and how for years she had found inspiration in a bottle. "You don't know how much courage it takes to be in the arts. Isn't there any part of you that can begin to forgive your father?"

Begin to forgive. . . . As she tucked Henry in at night, those words resonated. She loved Henry with all her soul, yet she was hardly a perfect mother. Who knows? Maybe someday Henry would have to forgive her. . . . And with that insight, for the first time, Ella felt her heart softening toward her father.

Sometimes Laurie didn't even need words to help Ella. Once Ella was walking down the street in the throes of craving a drink. Every bar she passed seemed to call her inside. I'll never make it home, she thought. I'm just not strong enough. As she felt herself giving way, she noticed a pleasant-looking woman walking toward her. It was Laurie. She smiled and gave her a little nod and walked on—but that was enough. Ella turned from the bar door and headed home.

After two years of hard-won sobriety, Ella finally felt strong enough to take the next step in her recovery—making amends to everyone she had ever wronged. The process was painful, but strangely exhilarating, too. As Ella sorted through her mental file of people she had mistreated, the image of Sofia deeply troubled her. At her next meeting, she stood up and spoke. "I grew up mostly abroad," Ella said. "My father left this country to paint, and he took us with him. And I was really raised by this wonderful peasant woman—Sofia, our housekeeper. My own parents were chaotic and crazy, but Sofia was very calm and kind. She gave me structure and rules that made sense. And I think that any sense of discipline that I've been able to find in myself these last two years to get sober, I owe to her.

"And I feel so bad because every Christmas, she writes and begs me to visit. And I never pay any attention to it. She retired and moved back to her little village, and I think she's lonely. And now I realize, she was like a mother to me. And if she wants me to visit, I should honor her by doing it. But I can't . . . I just can't. Because I'm so afraid." She paused, then caught Laurie's eye and gathered the resolve to continue.

"I'm just so scared that I won't find any meetings there. The only way I keep sober is by going to a meeting every single day. And they don't have support groups over there like we do here. And if I can't find one, I'll fall right back into the pit and wake up dead drunk and hate myself forever."

"Ella," said Laurie, "do you really think it's important that you go?"

"Yes."

"Then why don't you go?" said Laurie. "Just trust that if you need something badly enough, you'll get it."

Laurie's words convinced her. Ella made arrangements for Henry to stay with her sister, and she flew to Athens, Greece, her childhood home. As soon as she landed, she began searching for a support group meeting. To her amazement, she found one right away, located in the very church where she had been confirmed. The meeting wasn't until evening, and as Ella wandered the city, she became increasingly agitated. So many memories. . . . At lunch, the waiter poured a glass of wine without asking, and she almost drank it before she convinced him to take it away. By the time she entered the church for the meeting, she felt very frail and vulnerable. Her footsteps echoed off the marble floor as she slowly, self-consciously made her way to a seat. A dozen ravaged-looking old men turned to stare at her. She was the only woman there. Ella took her seat, aching with loneliness. Another set of footsteps echoed in the church. Ella turned to look—and there was Laurie.

"No!" Ella gasped. "It can't be!"

Laurie stared at her, eyes widening in shock. Then the two women fell into each other's arms.

"What are you doing here?" said Ella.

"Giving a concert. And going crazy trying not to drink!"

"I'm going crazy too!"

"Well, let's go crazy not drinking together."

That night, Ella couldn't sleep. She stared at the ceiling, marveling at the extraordinary coincidence that had brought Laurie and her together, thousands of miles from home. Was it mere chance, just a meaningless random event? Or was somebody upstairs working miracles on her behalf? Maybe she wasn't alone in her fight to stay sober. Maybe—was it possible?— she had magic on her side.

Over the next few days in Athens, Ella and Laurie helped each other stay the course. But as Ella's departure date loomed, she began to panic. The time had come to visit Sofia. That meant spending two weeks in a tiny, remote, unsophisticated mountain village. Forget about magic and miracles and anything else she'd been imagining. She would never, ever find a support group there.

"What'll I do?" she wailed to Laurie. "I've never gone a single day without a meeting."

"Remember what I told you," Laurie said gently. "Just trust that if you really need something badly enough, you'll get it."

With Laurie's words to comfort her, as always, Ella set out on her journey. She arrived at Sofia's doorstep, tired and anxious, still brooding about finding a meeting. Sofia rushed out and smothered her with kisses. "Come in, come in! I'm so happy you're here!"

Nervously, Ella followed Sofia inside. The first thing she noticed was a door on the right. Attached to the door was a golden plaque inscribed with the prayer of her support group.

"Sofia! Why do you have this here?" she exclaimed.

"Oh, that . . . the priest knows I have an empty room in my house, and he asked if he could use it for a kind of meeting that is called AA. Every night, people come to this room. Don't worry. They won't bother you."

"I'm not worried, believe me!" Ella threw her arms around Sofia, laughing. "Not worried at all. In fact, I think I'll join their meeting!"

Today, Ella is a confident young woman who has been sober for more than ten years. "When I look back at that trip," she says, "I can see it was the turning point. So much magic happened to me that I finally started to learn how to trust. Sometimes you need proof that you really will get what you need. That trip was my proof."

~ *Peggy Sarlin*

THE ANTIQUE GLASS

"*I*f I ever get remarried, all I want is a bridal shower!"

This was the one and only wish of my dear mother-in-law, who had been divorced for eight years. It must have been poignant for her to attend the bridal showers of her two son's brides—my sister-in-law and myself—in a solitarily single state. My heart ached for my mother-in-law when I heard her wonder out loud, "Will I ever have the opportunity to be as happy as my children?"

After marrying off two wonderful sons (one of whom is my husband) within the same year, my mother-in-law must have figured that three weddings is the charm. She finally met Mr. Right, and we all rejoiced for her. I also remembered the wistful request she had made so many months before, and I felt determined to fulfill it and throw her an unforgettable shower.

I went to work right away on arrangements. There were invitations to mail, chairs to rent, a house to clean, food to cook. This was going to be the party to surpass all parties . . . and a surprise one to boot. I wanted to make sure that every single detail would be perfect. To add some "class" to this special event, I borrowed party favors, accessories, and decorations from a friend of mine who was a professional party planner. As I left her home, my arms laden with bride-and-groom dolls, colored glasses, and wooden bird cages to decorate the table, my generous-spirited friend called after me, "Wait! There's one more thing I want to lend you."

It was her most prized possession—an antique oversized crystal champagne glass. The perfect centerpiece!

"I know how much this party means to you," she said, "so I really want it to be special. Please take this—but please remember to be extra careful with it. It's my favorite piece, and I was never able to find another one anywhere."

"You're a doll," I said gratefully. "What a friend! Don't worry; I'll guard it with my life."

I rushed home, thrilled to have such professional-looking accoutrements to dress up my party table. I couldn't contain my excitement for long, so I decided to set the table then and there—several days in advance of the party! When I finished, I stood back from the table and admired my handiwork. I called my husband into the dining room and got the kudos I had hoped to elicit. The table did indeed look very festive.

Soon, different family members (except for my mother-in-law, of course) trooped in for a tour of the much-touted table. "She's going to love it," my grandmother enthused, "especially that champagne glass. What a fabulous piece! She is going to be so surprised."

Two days before the bridal shower, however, that "surprise" was almost aborted when I got an unexpected call from my mother-in-law's fiancé. He and my mother-in-law were two minutes away by car, he said, and wanted to stop by and give my husband some old mail. Oh, no! I groaned inwardly. In a panic, I rushed to the dining room, swept everything off the table, and quickly crammed drawers and cabinets with the party stuff. As the doorbell rang, I reached for the last thing on the table—the champagne glass—and carefully put in on the floor of our walk-in storage closet. By the time I answered the door, not a single piece of "evidence" remained to testify to the big surprise that I was planning for that Sunday. My mother-in-law and her fiancé stayed for several hours, so I could not reset the table until the next morning.

I rushed around the dining room, pulling objects from their hiding places, duplicating my movements of the previous day, and all were going well until it was time to place the finishing touch on the table—the antique champagne glass. As I opened the storage closet to retrieve the glass, my heart sank when I saw it on the floor . . . broken. My heart began to pound and my face flushed in shame. *This is my favorite piece!* I could hear my friend saying. My own staunch reassurance—Don't worry; I'll guard it with my life!—came back to haunt me, in mockery. How could this have happened?

My father was the blameless culprit. He had opened the closet door earlier that morning in search of the vacuum cleaner and had accidentally stepped on the glass.

I tried to squelch the panic rising up in me, but I was utterly devastated by what had happened. Every single member of my extended family was enlisted to scour all of Manhattan's department and specialty stores (no mean feat) in search of a replica. But my friend had been quite correct in her assertion to me that she had never been able to find another one. Despite everyone's best attempts, the champagne glass couldn't be found anywhere.

"Don't worry," my husband said as he tried to calm me.

"God will reward you for being so kind to my mother—he will surely pay you back."

He was trying valiantly to alleviate my distress—which I appreciated, of course—but I could hardly believe that there was any way this awful scenario could improve.

I put my worries on the back burner when Sunday came, the day of the shower. My mother-in-law was genuinely surprised, quipping that she felt like a kid all over again as she eagerly opened her gifts with excitement and joy.

Cookbooks . . . pots . . . linens . . . everything a new bride needs and loves. I had never seen her happier. By all counts and everyone's standards, the bridal shower was a huge success. The antique champagne glass wasn't missed by anyone except me.

When the guests started to leave, the family members and friends who had graciously stayed behind to help began to fold the chairs and clear the table. It was then that a friend of my mother's, whom I did not even remember putting on the guest list, approached me and said, "I have a gift for you."

"For me?" I asked, confused. "You mean for my mother-in-law, right?"

"No, for you," she said. "I never attend a party without bringing a gift for the hostess." She handed me a gift-wrapped box, congratulated my mother-in-law once more, and left.

Later, when the house became quieter and most of the guests had left, I opened the box. Inside was an exact twin of the antique champagne glass!

I checked the invitation list. This woman's name was not on it.

"Things like this don't happen in real life," I said to my husband, who had tears in his eyes himself.

"God really does reward us in mysterious ways," he answered. "You did something very special for my mother and really made her feel good. In turn, God sent this woman to you to replace the broken glass. One good deed begets another!"

~ *C. Stern*

THE DREAM

*F*irst came the volley of shots, then the high-pitched screams, and finally, the irrevocable silence of death. Later, in the women's barracks, hushed whispers would tell of an aborted escape by some of the men. And much later, a young woman by the name of Esther would learn that Yidel—her beloved brother and only surviving family member—had been among the casualties.

Now her world was totally broken, destroyed. She was the last, the remnant. Two years earlier, when Hitler's nightmare had first been unleashed in Poland, her beloved parents had been shot down by the Nazis in cold blood, and Yidel—older by four years—had become both father and mother to her. Yidel had been her sanctuary and port, her stalwart companion during her sojourn through the camps. Now he was gone. She was twenty years old and completely alone.

"He died a hero," she tried to console herself. "And better a bullet in the back than death in the gas chambers." That ignoble death would soon be her fate, she was sure, when she discovered that the next stop on her journey was the infamous death camp Sobibór.

Until now, Esther had been relatively fortunate. Over the course of the past two years, she had been moved from camp to camp, but all of them had been "work" camps, where slave labor was harnessed for the Third Reich, where it was still possible to survive.

But Sobibór, like Treblinka and Belzec, was a "death camp." Its only industry was extermination. When Esther was told she would be transported to Sobibór, she knew the end was near. Sobibór existed for one purpose only—the manufacture of death.

Strangely, though, when she entered the main gate of Sobibór together with the crush of hundreds, it was a sense of elation, not despair, that suddenly engulfed her. "You are going to escape from here!" a voice deep inside her exulted. That certainty surged through her even as her eyes absorbed the impossibly high barbed wire fence, the formidable watchtowers that loomed overhead, the menacing guard dogs with bared teeth.

Her first minutes at the death camp served only to confirm her incongruous conviction that here at last, in the jaws of hell, she was going to be blessed. For whenever a new transport arrived, a selection was made. Almost all of the arrivals were sent immediately to the furnaces, but during each selection a handful were plucked out from the crowd and spared.

Sobibór was not only a death factory but also a place where Nazi personnel lived, and skilled laborers were required to tend to their needs and maintain the camp. Sometimes the call came for carpenters, or goldsmiths, or dentists; sometimes musicians, or singers, or dancers were recruited to entertain the Nazis when they were bored at night. On this particular day, the Nazi recruiter just happened to be looking for women who knew how to knit, a skill at which Esther excelled.

Out of the transport of eight hundred young people who arrived at Sobibór that day, only seven were selected for a temporary reprieve. And Esther was one of them.

"Eventually, they'll replace us with others," one inmate murmured to another.

"No one leaves here alive."

"We must escape!"

And so, almost as soon as she had arrived at the camp where her fate never looked bleaker and the odds never seemed greater, Esther joined with other feisty spirits to plot the famous Sobibór uprising of October 14, 1943—the largest prisoner escape of World War II.

On the eve of the revolt, Esther bade farewell to those in the barracks who would not be joining their effort to escape. They were either too sick or dispirited to try. We're never going to make it, either, Esther thought sadly as she kissed her friends good-bye. But better a bullet in the back than death in the gas chambers.

That night her sleep was restless and her dreams had a hallucinatory quality to them. In one of those dreams, she saw her deceased mother enter the main gate of Sobibór.

"Mama," she cried out in disbelief. "What are you doing here? Don't you know that we're going to escape tomorrow?"

"I know," her mother answered calmly. "That's why I came."

"Esther'le," her mother said tenderly, "I am here to tell you that you will escape! And this is where you must go when you do."

Her mother took her by the hand, led her out of the gate, and brought her to a barn. They went inside the barn, and there her mother pointed toward the loft and said in a clear, firm voice: "Here you'll go, and here you'll survive."

And then she disappeared.

Esther awoke with a start and, trembling, roused the woman

who shared her bunk. Shaking, Esther recounted the dream, but her friend was unimpressed and made short shrift of its import.

"Listen," she scoffed, "you're nervous, you're scared, of course you would dream about the escape. But the dream doesn't mean anything. Don't take it seriously."

Esther was unswayed by her friend's dismissive words.

"Nonetheless," she vowed, "if somehow I miraculously survive, I won't rest until I find the place my mother showed me!"

In the dream, Esther had recognized the barn; she actually knew the place quite well. As a child, she had tumbled in its hay and played hide-and-seek underneath its rafters. It was part of the property owned by a Christian farmer, a friend of her deceased father's, a kind man who lived eighteen kilometers away from her hometown of Chelm, a town that was currently occupied and flooded by legions of Nazi soldiers.

"This is the place you'd escape to?" Esther's friend asked incredulously. "You'd have to be crazy . . . walking into the enemy's embrace. You might as well die here!"

"My mother didn't come to me for nothing," Esther said stubbornly. "If she told me to go to the barn, there must be a good reason."

On the morning of October 14, some three hundred inmates of Sobibór, armed with weapons smuggled into the camp by sympathetic partisans, revolted. Chaos erupted as phone wires were snipped, electric cables cut, guards overwhelmed, the armory seized, Nazi soldiers shot, and hundreds of prisoners jumped the barbed wire fence. As Esther leaped to freedom and ran for cover to the adjoining woods, blood gushed from her scalp. She had always feared a bullet in her back; but when it came, it grazed her head instead.

Faint with hunger and weak from her injuries, Esther nonetheless prevailed. In the forest, she joined up with a group of partisans with whom she traveled. She hid by day and walked at night, and when the hunger and thirst drove her to the brink of madness, she knocked at the doors of the little farmhouses she passed, and mercifully, everyone was kind.

The partisans begged her to stay with them and become a permanent member of their group. She would be safer, much safer, they tried to convince her, if she hid in the woods and joined their cause. But Esther could not be deterred.

"I have to find the barn in the dream," she said stubbornly.

And two weeks later she did.

Beyond the edge of the woods where she walked, she finally saw the outlines of the structure she had so tenaciously sought. She waited until dusk, and then warily slipped inside. The barn was empty. She ascended the ladder to the loft, made a bed out of the hay, and then fell asleep.

The next day, she went hunting for food. A compassionate farmer gave her a loaf of bread and a bottle of milk, but when she returned to the loft to slowly savor her meal, an odd thing occurred. She placed the bottle of milk on top of a bale of hay while she tore into the bread, but when she turned to retrieve it, the bottle was gone. Somehow the mounds of hay enveloping her had swallowed the bottle up whole, or else it had dropped to the floor below. Esther was frantic with thirst. She dug through the hay and hunted on the floor. All sense of caution was flung aside as she clawed at the floorboards in vain, making agitated noises as she dove deeper into the hay. Her movements grew louder and more careless with each passing moment, jolting awake the slumbering figure huddled in a corner on the other side of the barn.

"Who's there?!" the figure sprang up in alarm.

Now I'm finished, Esther thought.

"Who's there?" the menacing figure shouted once more.

Esther froze in shock.

"Yidel?" she cried in disbelief as she recognized her brother's unmistakable voice. "Yidel . . . is that you?"

"Esther!" he screamed. "Esther'le!"

"But Yidel . . ." she labored slowly, incomprehensibly. "You're supposed to be dead!"

"No, Esther, you're the one who's dead!"

"They told me you were shot at the work camp . . . ," she said.

"Esther," he broke in gently, "I was the only one who escaped that night. Everyone else was killed. But Esther'le," he said, eyes brimming with tears, "someone told me that you were dead! I am overcome with joy that you are alive! But how did you know to come here?" Yidel asked in wonderment.

"Mama told me to," Esther explained. "She came to me in a dream. I'll tell you all about it soon. But first I want to know: How long have you been here?"

"Ten months. Papa's friend has been hiding me here since I escaped."

"Yidel!" Esther sobbed. "All I want you to do is sit with me all night and just hold my hand. . . . And then we'll watch the sun rise . . . together."

The next morning, the two heard a loud, sharp whistle coming from outside the barn. "That's a signal for me to come out," Yidel explained hurriedly to Esther.

"It's Papa's friend, the farmer. He wants to talk to me."

The eyes of the farmer were tense and worried.

"I don't know if I can keep you here anymore," he said not unkindly. "A strange woman has been seen wandering nearby, and no one knows if she belongs to a partisan group or who she is. I'm worried that the neighbors will get suspicious."

"That woman is my sister!" Yidel cried. And he told the farmer the miraculous story of his sister, the dream, and her escape from Sobibór.

The farmer was visibly moved by Yidel's account.

"Well, if God brought you together," he said, "who am I to tear you apart? Your sister can stay with you in the barn."

And in that barn, thanks to the loving guidance of a mother who watched over her children from a world beyond, Esther and Yidel hid safely for nine more months, until they were liberated by the Russians and the war finally ground to its end.

More than half-a-century later, there are very few survivors of Sobibór left to tell the story, and Esther and Yidel are among them. For the siblings, every day is a continuing celebration of the miracle of motherly love, a legacy that defies both time and memory.

~ Esther Raab, as told to the authors

A MYSTERIOUS JAM

*S*he had felt an immediate kinship with him and thought the feeling was mutual.

He had taken an instant dislike to her and couldn't wait to take her back home.

The hours flew by for her; time had never seemed to pass so quickly.

To him, every minute was an eternity.

She wished the night would never end.

He was sorry it had ever begun.

Still, he was a gentleman, and he didn't want to hurt her feelings. She was, after all, sweet and soft and kind—just not his type. He was attracted to women who were mysterious and aloof, confident and smug. The kind of women who never went out on blind dates set up by anxious friends. When he had called her on Monday, he had detailed his plans for the Saturday night date, seeking her approval. Dinner, a Broadway show, dancing at the new club everyone was raving about. He couldn't back out of any of it now; it would be too much of a rebuff. Her eyes lit up with joy as the evening stretched out before them; his glazed over with boredom.

Then the date was finally over. She sighed, Too bad; he breathed, Thank God! He drove her back to her home in Brooklyn and eagerly pushed the door handle on the driver's side so he could escort her inside.

There was one minor problem. The car door was jammed.

"That's weird," he muttered, consternation flooding his face as he tried to jimmy the handle open. It wouldn't budge.

He banged the door with his fist, kicked it with his foot, shoved it with his shoulder. To no avail. It was absolutely, positively, and very mysteriously, stuck. Flustered, he turned to her with his apologies. "Sorry," he said, "but we'll have to go out through the door on your side. Do you mind?"

She tugged at the handle, and he waited for the door to swing wide open, offering deliverance and escape.

Her door wouldn't budge, either.

"This is so bizarre!" he exclaimed. "We went in and out of the car at least a half dozen times tonight, and there was nothing wrong with either door. There wasn't even a hint of any problem. I just don't understand it. It's not as if it's icy outside or freezing. Why should the doors jam right now?"

The car was a two-door model. It was the middle of the night, and they were in the middle of a very quiet, middle-class Brooklyn neighborhood. The houses lining the block were dark; none blazed with light or life. Not a single soul seemed to be stirring on the sleepy, deserted street. It was in the days before cell phones, and as frantic for flight as he was, he knew it would be cruel and unfair to use his horn to signal trouble and wake up the sleeping residents. Deliverance from his date might have to be postponed awhile. "Well," he said, turning to her with a rueful smile, "I guess we'll just have to wait until someone drives by and rescues us. . . . I'm sure there are other young people on the block who stay out late on Saturday night."

"I don't know . . . ," she said hesitantly. "Most of the people living on this street are pretty elderly."

Inwardly, he shuddered. Outwardly, he flashed her a dazzlingly false grin that in her naiveté she took to be genuine.

"But hey," she said, brightening at the prospect of spending some more time with him, "we can get a chance to truly talk now. . . . The show and the dancing were great, but they didn't give us much time to really get to know each other. . . . So tell me," she said, turning to him with an open, interested smile, "what do you think of . . . ?"

Better make the best of it, he groaned, resigning himself to a few hours of boredom. But as she drew him into the conversation, he found himself increasingly enchanted by her candor, her little enthusiasms, her vivacity. She was intelligent, well read, easygoing. And she was, to be fair, a really good sport about the jammed doors. Maybe he had misjudged her. Maybe it had been unfair to dismiss her so quickly. Maybe first impressions weren't the right impressions, after all. Maybe he would even ask her out . . . again.

It's been ten years since that fateful night, and they've been happily married for the last nine and a half.

They never could figure out why the car doors jammed that night, but actually, in retrospect, they're glad they did.

~ *Yitta Halberstam*

THE BRIS

*W*hen the blizzard of '56 hit New Haven, dumping an unprecedented twenty-five inches of snow, schoolchildren squealed with delight. School was canceled for days on end, and the city ground to a virtual halt. The children pulled out their rusty sleds from basement storage spaces and frolicked in the snow, while in the municipal garages the city's snowplows stood helpless. Adults, liberated from grueling routine, welcomed the respite, excited at the winter wonderland that had descended on them. But inside one house, a woman peered anxiously outside as the snow continued to fall.

Sarah Chanowitz had given birth to her first and only son one week before. As is customary in Jewish homes, the male infant was to be named—and circumcised—in a religious ceremony called a "bris." It was a momentous event in the life of a Jew—a major milestone of ritual consecration, a significant rite of passage in which family and community were expected to participate joyously.

But all night long, the snow had continued to fall unabated, and by morning the streets had not been cleared. The city had been rendered immobile, its public transportation system completely crippled.

For two days and nights, Mrs. Chanowitz had cleaned and scoured, peeled and grated, cooked and baked—and a dazzling display of delicacies and confections covered her dining room and kitchen tables. But now she wondered: Would anyone be able to come to the bris?

Her closest friends lived far away. Men tended to be more stalwart about trudging through drifts, mounds, and hills of snow . . . she was sure that at least the required minyan (a quorum of ten men) would faithfully appear. But how many women would brave the dizzying white of the day? How many women could she count on to attend this most momentous event, one in which she longed for some female companionship?

Miraculously, there were three. Three intrepid souls who knew how much their presence—or absence—would mean to Sarah Chanowitz. Three steadfast, loyal, tenacious women who slipped, skidded, and stumbled their way to Mrs. Chanowitz's door, wet snow clinging to their hair, faces, and clothing, laughing as they tramped inside and shook themselves free of the snow.

"Why, Judy Herman*!" Sarah shouted, jubilant, when she spotted her first friend. "I can't believe it . . . you live a mile away!"

"I wouldn't miss your son's bris for anything!" Judy smiled, bending over to give Sarah a wet kiss.

"Sadie Glick!" Sarah exclaimed a few minutes later when she saw her close friend framed in the doorway. "I thought you were still recovering from the minor surgery you had last week!"

"Wild horses couldn't keep me away!" Sadie laughed, enfolding her friend in a warm embrace.

* The names Judy Herman, Sadie Glick, and Miriam Segal are pseudonyms.

"Miriam Segal, is that really you . . . or is it a mirage?" Sarah whooped again in excitement a few minutes later. "How on earth did you get here? You live almost two miles away!"

"Hey, Sarah," Miriam laughed, "I'd walk halfway across the world for you, don't you know that?"

These were the three women who showed, and Sarah felt loved and grateful. She knew what a tremendous sacrifice they had made for her, and she felt blessed to have such loving friends.

But as it turned out, Sarah wasn't the only one to be blessed that day. It seems that her little house, so radiant with joy, so aglow with love, and so luminous with the warmth of special friends, had become a vessel that day—a cornucopia of blessings that filled up, overflowed, and inundated all those within its reach.

Nine months after her own son's bris, Sarah Chanowitz was kept busy one morning rushing to three different brises taking place all over town.

Her first stop was a local synagogue where the Herman family's bris was being held. Judy Herman had had six little girls in rapid succession; this was her first son.

Next Sarah headed for a small catering hall where the Glick bris was taking place. Sadie Glick had had two children—now teenagers—and then none had followed; she had been suffering from secondary infertility and had been unable to conceive another child for the last eight years.

Miriam Segal had been childless for ten. The Segal bris that Sarah attended later that morning was perhaps the most joyous affair of all.

Nine months after they had attended the Chanowitz bris and drunk from the goblet that contained the ritual wine used in the ceremony, all three women—Judy Herman, Sadie Glick, and Miriam Segal—bore sons and had bris ceremonies of their own.

Sarah Chanowitz had always felt indebted to the three and wished she could repay their extraordinary kindness. Miraculously, it seemed, she had accomplished her goal.

~ Sarah Chanowitz, as told to the authors

RED COWGIRL BOOTS

My granddaughter Tate turned five years old recently, and her mother gave her a very special present: a pair of red cowgirl boots that had been her own when she was a little girl. Tate pulled on the little red boots and began to dance around the room. It is always fun to dress up in Mom's clothes when you are a little girl, but when Mom's clothes are your own size, well, the excitement is almost uncontainable.

Kelly, my daughter-in-law, told us about the first time she wore her boots. You see, not only did she experience the thrill of wearing her first pair of real cowgirl boots; she also experienced the thrill of meeting her first love.

She was five and he was seven. He lived in the city, and his father brought him to Kelly's grandfather's farm one Saturday afternoon to ride the horses. Kelly sat on the top fence rail as Grandfather saddled her pony. She was trying very hard not to get her shiny new boots dirty when the city boy came over to say hello. He smiled at her and admired her new boots. It must have been love at first sight, because Kelly offered to let him ride her pony. She had never let anyone ride her pony before.

Later that year, Grandfather sold the farm, and Kelly didn't see the young boy again. But Kelly never forgot that magical moment in her childhood, and she thought of the city boy every time she put on her red cowgirl boots. When she outgrew them, her mother packed them away. Years later, while organizing for a garage sale, Kelly found the little red boots and decided to give them to Tate for her birthday.

Tate's laughter brought us back to the present. My son, Marty, scooped his giggling daughter into his arms and danced around the room with her. "I do like your new cowgirl boots, baby," he said. "They remind me of the day I rode my very first pony. I wasn't much older than you."

"Is this a true story, Daddy? Or a make-believe one?" Tate loved to listen to her daddy tell stories about when he was a little boy. "Does it have a happy ending?" Then she begged him to tell her about his first pony ride. Marty smiled at Tate's unending string of questions as he sat down in the big, comfortable recliner. Tate climbed up into his lap.

"Once upon a time when I was seven years old, I lived in the big city called St. Louis. That's in Missouri. I wanted a horse more than anything in the world, but we couldn't have one in the city. I told my dad that I wanted to be a real cowboy when I grew up, so that summer he took me to a farm not very far from here. And I got to ride a real pony for the very first time."

You can guess how Marty's story ends, but as incredible as it sounds, Marty and Kelly had no idea they had met as children until the day of their daughter's fifth birthday.

True stories have happy endings, too!

~ *Jeannie Williams*

THE ULTIMATE GIFT

Hospital waiting rooms may vary in size and decor, but in atmosphere they're all basically the same. The mood is tense, serious, fearful. People pace nervously, glance at their watches; they stare into space; they weep quietly. The waiting room is the place where destinies change forever. And it's the place where Caroline Matthews* met Bill Gardner for the first time on a cold January morning.

The hospital had waiting rooms on every floor, but both had separately chosen to retreat to the first-floor visitors' atrium. Caroline was huddled in a corner, crying softly; Bill, watching from afar, was struck by her despair. Most people steer clear of their weeping neighbors, but Bill Gardner reached out. "What's the matter?" he gently asked, leaning toward Caroline compassionately.

"It's my mother," she sobbed. "She's been here since October waiting for a heart transplant. If she doesn't get one soon, she'll die."

Caroline's mother, Barb, was fifty-six years old and had had a massive heart attack in October. She had been confined to the cardiac care unit of the hospital ever since, waiting for a heart that would match her blood type and size. She had been added to a waiting list that stretched four thousand names long, and the odds were that she would die before the perfect match was found for her.

* The names in this story, a dramatization, are pseudonyms.

Throughout her life, Barb had been extraordinarily devoted to her daughter, who was now thirty-one. When Caroline's first marriage had failed, Barb had taken her daughter and grandchild into her home until the two had been able to get back on their feet. Caroline couldn't bear the thought of her mother slipping away from her like this. Her mother had to live; she needed her mother to live!

After pouring her heart out to Bill Gardner and being comforted by his empathy, Caroline noticed his own dazed and stricken look. The emotional combat fatigue straining his features indicated that he was not an expectant father eagerly awaiting news of the birth of his child. Something far more serious had brought him to this waiting room today, Caroline realized—so, gently, she too made inquiries.

"My wife has a rare brain defect," he answered, "but the doctors say they can treat it. She should be out of here in a week."

Janie Gardner had always been healthy and robust, but a few weeks earlier she had suddenly begun experiencing debilitating headaches. Then she had had a grand mal seizure that brought her to the hospital. A CAT scan revealed the startling news that the thirty-eight-year-old woman had been born with an arteriovenous malformation—a rare brain defect that deprives the brain of blood—and that she had been living on borrowed time.

"My God," a radiologist gasped when he read the CAT scan. "How has this woman been able to survive all these years?"

The defect was so advanced that the only option now was a twenty-seven-hour, two-part operation, but doctors were confident that it would be successful and that Janie would make a complete recovery. Caroline was happy, for Bill's sake, that the prospects for his wife's recovery were good. By contrast, her own mother's chances for survival grew slimmer every day.

After a long conversation, Caroline and Bill finally rose from their seats in the visitors' lounge, bade each other good luck, and said good-bye. They never expected to see each other again.

But over the next few days, they kept running into each other. They always seemed to be headed for the same bank of elevators, the same hospital corridor, or the same waiting room at the exact same time. And soon they developed a special bond, as they tried by turns to support one another, offer hope, and provide cheer. Bill spoke often of his and Janie's four children; Caroline shared stories about her son. And they promised each other that, when their loved ones finally recovered and were discharged, they'd all go out together and celebrate.

But one morning, Caroline entered the atrium and found the usually optimistic Bill dissolved in tears. In the aftermath of the operation, it seemed, Janie's brain had started hemorrhaging. She was now in a coma and on life support.

Each day after that, Bill provided Caroline with updates whenever they encountered one another. And by now they were running into each other so regularly that each no longer feigned surprise when they saw the other in the lounge.

"Janie's coming out of the coma!" Bill told Caroline excitedly one day. "I read her a get-well card that our daughter Tess had sent, and tears rolled down her face as I read it. And then . . . Tess had asked at the end: 'Mommy, if you like this card, please squeeze Daddy's hand.' And she did! Janie squeezed my hand!"

He added, "The doctors say that Janie's making rapid strides, and we should begin discussing plans for rehabilitation soon."

But a few weeks later, the worst-case scenario for Janie Gardner occurred. Her brain ruptured, in what doctors call a "lethal bleed." This time, there was nothing that they could do but helplessly watch her fade away.

Two days later, Bill Gardner finally faced the truth: This time, there would be no miraculous recoveries, no sudden reversals, no inexplicable changes-for-the-better. Janie was on an irrevocable journey toward death.

And it was then that Bill, who always thought of other people first—even in the throes of deepest grief—thought of seeking out the nurse in charge of organ donations.

Janie had always been a fervent exponent of organ donation. She believed that donating your organs was a way of doing service —a final gift to the world from beyond the grave. Bill knew that Janie would want him to proceed with the plan he had just outlined in his head.

Bill found the nurse in charge of organ donations and made his unusual request. He wanted to donate his wife's organs when she expired. She nodded. But Janie's heart, he added—he wanted to donate her heart to someone specific. . . . Could that be done? The nurse stared at him, nonplussed.

Direct donations of organs to specific recipients was almost unheard-of, she explained. In fact, she had never seen it done. But technically, she didn't see why it couldn't be done. She hastily referred him to the medical director of cardiac transplantation and the director of heart and lung transplantation. They had performed countless transplant operations, but none like the one Bill Gardner had in mind. The doctors told Bill that the chances of the matches being perfect, in terms of organ and body size, were about one in a million.

But Bill Gardner was not discouraged, nor was he deterred by the daunting statistics. Caroline Matthews had opened his heart to the plight of her mother. And now he wanted to bequeath to her the ultimate gift of his heart—the one belonging to his cherished wife.

As doctors made arrangements for organ matching tests, Bill raced downstairs to the visitors' atrium where he was certain he would find Caroline. At first, she couldn't comprehend what Bill was telling her. She cried on hearing that Janie was near death. And she cried even more when Bill told her that he wanted to give Janie's heart to Caroline's mother. "No one has ever given me a gift like this before," she sobbed.

Miraculously, Janie Gardner's heart proved to be a perfect match for Caroline's mother. Barb underwent the successful operation on February 14—Valentine's Day.

At Janie Gardner's funeral a few days later, the Gardner children sang their favorite song from the movie *Titanic*—Celine Dion's beloved "My Heart Will Go On."

~ *Judith Leventhal*

LURED INTO DAWN

*T*stared hard at the old color photograph, a deep yearning welling up inside me. The young girl burst joyously from the water. As she opened her eyes, a look of utter surprise lit up her face. Because directly in front of her, suspended in mid-air, was a large, sleek bottlenose dolphin. That young girl was me. And after all these years I was still in love with dolphins.

Now, twenty-three years later, sitting alone in my tiny, one bedroom Manhattan apartment, I felt utterly miserable. Where had my dream gone? What happened to that fiery passion?

Perhaps it was all the disappointments. At seventeen, I wrote letters to every marine biologist in the country, begging for an opportunity to be with dolphins. "Your enthusiasm is refreshing," they wrote back, "but we can't help." At nineteen, I dropped out of college and moved to Florida to try to get hired by the Miami Seaquarium as one of those "sea maids" who smile a lot and toss the dolphins fish. Every day I rode my bike to the Seaquarium, and every day they'd say, sorry, there are no openings at the moment. Eventually, I returned home defeated. With no handsome men banging down my door, I became self-sufficient as a writer.

But my love for dolphins never diminished. I began writing romance novels, and the one that did the best was published in 1981 and translated into seven languages. It was titled *Lured into Dawn* and written under the pen name Catherine Mills. It told the story of a New York businesswoman who falls madly in love with a dolphin trainer. While the heroine, Melinda Matthews, didn't exactly resemble me—she was tall, lithe, blonde, and the CEO of a successful New York cosmetics company, while I'm short, chunky, brunette, and deeply in debt—at least we shared common initials—MM. During a business trip to the lush island of Jamaica, she meets the ruggedly handsome Richard Carson, a seasoned dolphin trainer who worked at Sea Life Park, Jamaica—a fictional Montego Bay aquarium I made up out of my imagination. Of course in the end, they live happily ever after on a lush tropical island. The opening of the book describes their first unforgettable encounter. A frisky dolphin in a petting pool splashes Melinda, drenching her from head to toe. With her expensive silk dress clinging provocatively to her body, Melissa blushes beet red when she looks up and notices Richard staring at her. You can guess what happens after that . . .

Yet despite the book's international success, here I was, almost ten years later, living alone in a noisy city crowded with eight million people and not one single dolphin (or ruggedly handsome boyfriend) in sight.

One warm summer night, I was absolutely miserable, feeling as if I had made an irrevocable mistake in my life. The only remnants of my passion were dolphin posters covering my stark white walls and a few ceramic dolphin knickknacks collecting dust on my shelves. Somehow I had come to the painful realization that I never wanted to be a writer. That I didn't want to live alone in a big city. What I deeply wanted was to live by the sea, with a man I totally loved and admired, surrounded by those warm-blooded mammals who felt like my true family.

As the clock approached midnight, I lay awake feeling sorry for myself. I was too old to move to Miami and become a sea maid. Who would hire a chunky lady in her late thirties! I didn't want to become a biologist. All I wanted was to be with dolphins, the way you want to be near people you love.

Out of desperation, I called out to God. In the past, in times of deep need, God had come through for me, though always in ways I least expected.

"Please God," I whispered, "help me be with dolphins."

I slept late the next day. By the time I got up, it was near 11 a.m. Outside the skies were heavy with the threat of rain. As I sat dunking my tea bag into my dolphin ceramic mug, I suddenly heard a voice. "Go to the New York Aquarium," it said. Puzzled, I looked around. The voice wasn't exactly outside of me, but it wasn't inside, either. What a silly idea, I thought. The New York Aquarium was in Coney Island, Brooklyn. The neighborhood turned dangerous after dark, and it took hours to get there by subway. Besides, I thought, all it had were a bunch of fish behind glass walls. I went back to sipping my tea. But again the voice intruded. "Go to the New York Aquarium."

Yet still I argued against it. I don't know how to get there. It's too far and too late to go. When the voice loudly insisted a third time, I jumped to my feet. "All right!" I shot back. I called the aquarium, got directions, and reluctantly left the house.

A few hours later, I hurried to the entrance, paid my fee, and wandered inside. After walking through a dark corridor filled with fish tanks I found myself standing in front of a large outdoor aquatheater. And there, just beyond the low metal gate, splashing around in a large concrete pool, were three bottlenose dolphins. My heart nearly burst with joy. God had led me to the only dolphins in New York!

The next show wasn't for forty minutes so I climbed to the top of the bleachers and watched, mesmerized, as the dolphins entertained me. Minutes later, a young man in a red T-shirt emblazoned with the words "New York Aquarium" entered the aquatheater. He was busying himself with some task when suddenly the voice returned, pushier than ever. "Go talk to him." Instinctively I resisted. No way, I thought. "Go talk to him!" the voice insisted again. I felt stupid and shy. What would I say to him? But when the voice intruded a third time, I stood up and headed over to him. "Excuse me," I said to the young man, not having any idea what I was going to say. "Do you . . . uh . . . work with these dolphins?" Before long we were having a conversation about a volunteer program where people could assist the dolphin trainers.

He might as well have told me I won the million-dollar lottery. I could barely contain my excitement. "Don't get your hopes up," he urged, "volunteering is not about playing with dolphins. They hardly ever let you near them. They're extremely picky about who gets chosen."

Well, he could have said I needed to scale Mount Everest. Somehow I would have found a way. Needless to say, I got hired to work every Wednesday. It didn't matter that I'd have to leave Manhattan before dawn. It didn't matter that I'd have to stand on my feet eight hours a day in a stainless-steel feed room, defrosting hundreds of pounds of frozen mackerel, cleaning out plastic buckets thick with fish blood, or hauling large garbage bags of trash. What mattered was I knew my dolphins were always nearby.

Those Wednesdays changed my life. When friends saw me at a party a few weeks later, they said, "You look great. Are you in love?" Yes, I'd reply. Because it is not what happened with those friendly, warm-blooded dolphins—but with a friendly, hot-blooded dolphin trainer named Dennis Aubrey. He was one of the senior dolphin and whale trainers at the aquarium. A former New York businessman who had grown up in Key Largo, Florida, Dennis had sold his successful business to pursue his childhood dreams, which included buying a sailboat and becoming a dolphin trainer. The moment I laid eyes on him, the very instant we met, my heart did this sort of flip. Dennis made me nervous—women seemed to flock around him so I kept my distance. Despite that, every Wednesday we'd end up chatting and often working near each other. As the weeks passed, Dennis and I began flirting more and more. I never once thought about my old romance novel, *Lured into Dawn*—until the day Dennis pushed me into the dolphin pool. I was laughing so much that it wasn't until I climbed out and stood up that I realized he was staring at me. My clothes (not exactly a silk dress but a cotton New York Aquarium T-shirt and shorts) clung to me a bit too provocatively for my comfort. I blushed beet red. Gee, I thought, this feels strangely familiar. That's when it hit me. This was practically the opening scene in my very own book!

Soon afterward, I came into the aquarium one morning to see Dennis, in the distance, surrounded by a group of young school kids. Very often classes would tour our marine mammal department as part of a school trip. As I stood there watching him, he joked and chatted and laughed with the children. Gosh, I thought, he's so sweet and gentle. He'd make a great husband. Then it dawned on me: I wrote this scene, too!

Suffice to say, within the year we were engaged. In fact, our engagement party was actually at the New York Aquarium! A few weeks later, on a whim, we moved to Hawaii. That's when I found out that the fictional aquarium I had created for Richard Carson in Montego Bay wasn't fictional at all. The state of Hawaii had its own large marine life park called—you guessed it—Sea Life Park, Hawaii.

Three years after arriving in Hawaii, Dennis and I were married on the private island of Lanai, home to a large group of Pacific spinner dolphins. We lived on this small, rural island for almost four years, swimming sometimes daily with those magnificent wild dolphins. God had made my dream come true. I was living by the sea, with a man I deeply loved and admired, surrounded by my ocean family. And just like my romance novel, with God's continued blessing, we'll keep living happily ever after.

~ Marcia Mager

THE NEW POSITION

*T*he ad in the paper caught my attention immediately. "Director of Programming is sought for a women's organization to create and coordinate conferences, symposiums, book and author luncheons, etc.," it read. "Knowledge of current affairs and contemporary literature necessary. Experience required." My heart began to thump with excitement. "Yes!" I thought with growing elation. "This is it! This is the job I've been seeking for so long. I can feel it beckoning to me. This is it. . . . I just know it!" There was only one minor hitch: I didn't have the experience.

For years, I had worked in the public relations field as a writer, and I felt burnt out. In 1991, I was ready for a change but was beginning to learn that it's not so easy to switch careers, especially without retraining. I had been casting about for something to do that would tap into my skills and expertise when I saw the ad. This job sounded perfect. I was an inveterate lecture-attender and a voracious reader. Putting together lectures and seminars didn't sound difficult; it sounded like fun! But how was I going to circumvent the "experience required" part? First things first: I called the number in the ad and talked my way into an interview.

My interviewers were impressed with my credentials but concerned about my lack of programming experience. I assured them that I could handle the demands of the position, and they were swayed by my confidence. I got the job.

But my confidence foundered almost as soon as I arrived at the office on the first day. "Oh, so you're Helene Isaacs's successor," one elderly employee said with concern. "What big shoes to fill. She was a phenomenon!" Another said tactlessly, "Well, I do feel sorry for you. There's nobody in this world like Helene Isaacs!" Then a third remarked, "Well, a hearty welcome to our organization, which, you'll find, is a great place to work." Then she shook her head mournfully. "But it sure hasn't been the same since Helene Isaacs left!"

I was ready to pick up my purse and flee. How was I ever going to compete with the phantom Helene?

Then I was ushered into my predecessor's office and didn't know whether to laugh or cry. A veritable paper mountain of letters, memos, brochures, and newspaper clippings covered Helene's desk. "Uh . . . why don't you spend the day cleaning off Helene's desk," suggested the personnel director, embarrassed, hastily backing out of the room. "She was very brilliant and creative but a trifle . . . disorganized," she said in explanation as she retreated.

I put down my handbag and stared in dismay at the daunting paper mountain. What a way to begin! How was I expected to know which papers should be saved and which could be discarded? Couldn't this venerable icon at least have had the decency to clean off her desk before she left? I sighed. Just then, another staff member stuck her head into my room and said, "Oh, you're Helene's replacement; I want to welcome you. Helene was here eighteen years, you know. Do you think you could stay that long?"

I didn't think I could stay for another hour. I picked up the phone and called my friend Rose. "This was a terrible mistake!" I wailed. "How could I have had the nerve to even think for a minute that I could undertake a job for which I have no real experience! I never coordinated an all-day conference before. . . . I must have been out of my mind to think I could do it. I better get out of here fast before they discover what a hoax, what a charlatan, what a fraud I really am. In fact, I think I'm actually going to pick up my handbag and go home right now!"

"Whoa! Wait a minute!" cautioned my friend. "Where's the fearless 'can-do' spirit that's always infused your life? Where's your desire to stretch, to expand? Where's the woman I know and love who welcomes a challenge and a chance to grow? You can do it! All beginnings are hard."

"Yeah, you're right," I conceded sheepishly. "I shouldn't give up so fast. But what about this pile of papers I have to contend with?" I moaned. "What am I going to do with those?"

"Hey," Rose said, "why don't you look at it as a learning experience? Work your way through the stack very slowly, read each paper carefully, and by the time you're finished, I bet you'll know much more about the job than you did when you started."

I was inspired and heartened by her attitude. "You're right!" I exclaimed. "I'm going to see this as a challenge and a learning experience. I won't throw in the towel!" Blinking back my tears, I concentrated on going through the pile of papers stacked high on the desk.

When I finally got to the very last one, I blinked again. But this time it was in wonder and awe.

I picked up the old, yellowing, tattered piece of paper, dated, incredibly, 1956, and, shaking my head in amazement, knocked on a colleague's door. "Can I help you?" she asked cheerfully.

"Can you tell me who this woman was?" I asked, pointing to the paper. "In the first paragraph, she's identified as Judith Mandelbaum, but in the third paragraph she's referred to as Mrs. Mordechai Mandelbaum."

"Oh, Judith Mandelbaum—she was director of programming, too. She was Helene's predecessor, and she was excellent! She retired in 1962, when Helene took over. She was an icon of the organization, and she was here for ages!"

I returned to my office, smiling and relieved. And I knew . . . everything would work out fine, everything would be all right. I would meet the challenge of my new position, and I would succeed. I would be here for a while, I was sure.

You see, my own English first name is Judith; my husband's is Mordechai. And our family name is . . . Mandelbaum!

It's five years now, and I'm still at the job.

~ *Yitta Halberstam*

THE RETURNED PURSE

*T*he most beautiful summers take place in the Niagara region, and often the streets in the area's towns are filled with tourists and city folk. So it was nothing short of a miracle that it was a conscientious, kind-hearted local who found the lump in the road.

Brian was driving his truck down the familiar streets of his beloved hometown when he spotted something large lying in the middle of the road. Rather than swerve around it, as many motorists before him already had, he slowed his truck to take a closer look. When he reached the mysterious object, he saw that it was a woman's purse. Probably left it on the hood of her car and unknowingly drove off, he deduced.

Whoever the owner is, she must be frantic by now, Brian thought. He pulled his truck to the side of the road, dashed into the flow of traffic, and retrieved the purse. When he arrived home, he looked through the contents of the purse in the hope of finding the owner's identification. He found a wallet with a woman's name and phone number inside and dialed the number. The woman on the other end was extremely thankful for his kind deed, and she asked if she could pick up her purse that evening. Brian politely offered to drop it off himself.

He returned the purse to the young woman, a student who attended the university in the nearby city of St. Catharines. Brian had deduced correctly: She had indeed left the purse on the hood of her car and driven off absentmindedly. She thanked Brian profusely and searched through the purse to see if anything was missing. Fortunately, even after the spill on the road, all the items were present except for her student ID card. She was a little disappointed that she had lost the identification she needed to take her exams but still extremely grateful for the safe return of everything else. She thanked Brian again and said good-bye.

Several days later, Brian went to visit his brother Chris. As he walked up Chris's driveway, he noticed that his brother was talking with a young woman. As Brian approached the two, he realized that it was the owner of the purse—the same young woman he had seen days earlier. A look of confusion crossed his face, and the young woman looked equally confused.

Astonished to see her, he asked why she was at his brother's house. She in turn was dumbfounded to learn that Chris and Brian were brothers.

"Your brother just called me," she explained to Brian. "While he was driving his car down the highway this morning, he noticed something strange on the road. He stopped to retrieve it, and now I've come to pick it up."

Brian's brother had found her student card—the only missing item from the purse.

They all shared a laugh; she thanked the brothers again and left, all the original items in her purse now back and intact.

~ *Katrina M. Ratz*

LIFELINE

"*L*iz?" the slurred voice asked.

It was an early Wednesday morning in January 1999, and the officers of the securities lending firm on Wall Street were bracing for a busy day.

Stockbroker Liz H. always had a phone glued to her ear at that time of day, sometimes fielding several phone calls at once. When the phone rang and she heard herself addressed by name, she was sure that the call was from a client. But as the caller continued to speak, Liz began to realize that something was wrong. The woman's speech was garbled and incoherent. This woman is either loaded or stoned, Liz thought. And she's surely not a client.

Who could it be?

Liz didn't hang up, because she had a relative in trouble. "Someone in my family was having problems at the time," she recalls, "and I assumed that it must be her. I didn't recognize the voice, but I thought *Hey, when you're drunk or drugged you don't sound like yourself anyway.*" But after several minutes passed, Liz realized that it was a complete stranger, not a relative, who was on the other end of the line.

It's a wrong number, she thought, grasping the situation at last. And this woman is in trouble!

Liz frantically motioned a coworker, Em, to her side and whispered, "I don't know what's going on here, but I think you should pick up the other phone and listen. What do you think we should do?"

Em raced to the extension and eavesdropped on the conversation. From across the room she frantically mouthed a message to Liz: "We have to get her name and address. This sounds like an emergency!"

Meanwhile, the usually busy offices of the firm were strangely quiet. The ordinary constant jangle of the telephones would surely have been distracting for the women, if not tempting. But on this particular morning the phones were uncharacteristically dead, giving the two stockbrokers the time and slack to talk to the stranger on the phone.

"Pretend you're the Liz she knows," Em told her friend as she covered the phone with her hand. "If she realizes she has the wrong number, she may hang up. And then God knows what will happen."

"No one loves me. I cannot go on anymore," the stranger cried over the phone.

It was a delicate situation. The two stockbrokers desperately needed to extract information from the woman that could lead police to her home. But if the unknown "Liz" was a friend of the woman's, she wouldn't need to ask for such information. How to identify the woman without making her unduly suspicious?

"You know," Liz said ingenuously, "we have such a terrible connection, I can hardly hear you! Who is this? Your voice sounds so faint. Give me your number and I'll call you right back."

But forty-five minutes went by before they succeeded

in obtaining her number, and all the while the two women steadfastly kept the caller on the line.

"Sometimes all we heard was dead air," Liz remembers, "as the woman drifted in and out of consciousness. Em—whom I call the queen of shmoozing—was just great. She wouldn't give up. She kept maintaining the conversation with the woman and didn't let her get off the phone."

Finally, the woman gave them a jumble of phone numbers.

As Liz wrote them down, she frowned.

There are too many numbers here, she thought. Then consciousness dawned. Maybe three of those numbers were an area code!

Had the woman called long distance?

"She's calling from Virginia!" she whispered a few minutes later to Em. As Em kept her talking on the other phone, Liz called the local police.

And Em was still talking to her when the squad car arrived at the scene.

The police officers pounded on the locked door, but got no response. Then they tried the windows, but they were shuttered tight.

Just then, a neighbor dashed out the door of an adjoining house and raced over to the men.

"I've got her key," she said breathlessly.

When the police entered the woman's bedroom, they found her lying on the bed, unconscious. Her night table was littered with vials of prescription drugs and bottles of alcohol. They were all empty.

The telephone receiver was gripped tight in her motionless hand.

An officer picked up the phone. Em was still on the other end.

"Who are you?" he asked.

"We're the wrong number that she called!" the stockbroker replied.

In reflecting on the strange turn of events that led the two women to save the stranger's life four states away, Liz says, "It was just not her day to die! Everything conspired against it. First, she calls a Liz in Virginia and reaches instead a Liz in New York. Then the office goes strangely quiet so we have the time and ability to help her. A neighbor appears on the porch with the key just in the nick of time. And finally, the woman falls unconscious just seconds before the police arrive! Talk about timing! . . . But what's most amazing of all to me is that she asked for Liz. You pay attention when someone calls you by your name. If she had called and asked for 'Chrissie' instead of 'Liz,' I would in all probability have just hung up, and that woman would surely be dead."

~ *Judith Leventhal*

THE NEW KID

*I*n September 1995, my eight-year-old son came home from school one day to report excitedly that a new kid from overseas had just joined his class.

This kid, he told me happily, "is just like me in every way. It's really cool, Mom," he said. "Josh loves basketball, he's great at sports, he's mischievous, he's funny, and he knows how to play great tricks on the teachers!" (Terrific! Now the poor souls would have to contend with a devilish duo instead of just one menace who had previously operated solo!) Sure enough the two fun-loving, spirited imps teamed up for a series of high jinks, innocent pranks, and frolicking escapades that had the school staff reeling. My son was ecstatic about his new friend. "It's amazing how much he's like me," he constantly commented, in a tone of wonderment and delighted surprise.

One day, my son came home with Josh to work on a school project together. Since he lived in a different neighborhood, Josh asked if I could drive him home when they were done, and I readily agreed. When I pulled up at his address, he asked if I would like to come in and meet his mother. The hour was late, but never one to rebuff a child, I obligingly climbed out of the car. Josh ushered me into the living room and went to find his mother. "Eli's mother is here!" I heard him call to her. "Come meet her . . . you'll love her!"

Quick, light footsteps danced down the stairs, and I turned to meet Josh's mother. She blinked. I blinked. Her jaw dropped. My mouth gaped open. Her eyes filled with tears. I tried hard to muffle a sob. Then we simultaneously ran toward each other and embraced for a long time.

Josh stood staring at this scene transfixed and perplexed. "What's going on?" he asked.

"Oh, Josh!" his mother exclaimed laughing, wiping away a tear. "Eli's mother and I were best friends in high school. After graduation, I moved abroad, and I met Dad and lived overseas for years. I haven't seen Yitta for twenty-two years!"

Of course, I hadn't had an inkling. How could I have known? It was his father's surname—"Goodfriend"—that Josh used, not his mother's maiden name, although perhaps, on second thought, the name should have provided me with a slight suspicion, if not a telltale clue!

~ *Yitta Halberstam*

A PAIR OF SHOES

*J*osephine* had been blessed with two biological off-
spring of her own, but one day she told her husband
Frank that she wanted to adopt a child. She had just participated
in a massive clothing drive that her church had sponsored for
orphan children in China, and their plight moved her.

She wanted to do more than just send used clothing to
Chinese orphanages, she said with emotion. Helping these
abandoned and deprived children, she felt, meant reaching out
in a very real and concrete way. And in Josephine's mind, the
only way to truly make a difference in an orphan child's life was
to adopt that child and bring him or her into the permanent
sanctuary of her home. This was how she believed she could
genuinely salvage a broken soul.

Fortunately, her husband was as idealistic as she and he
agreed to the plan. They contacted the right agencies, filled
out the necessary paperwork, and traveled the great distance to
China from their home in Canada to claim their child. From the
mainland, they journeyed to a small village where their child
was housed, and it was many hours before they reached their
final destination.

Upon their arrival at the orphanage—one of thousands
scattered throughout the country—the fragile little boy who
would soon be theirs was brought to meet them for the first

* The names in this story are pseudonyms.

time. As Josephine gazed at him tenderly, something about the child's appearance caught her eye. She gasped, and tears flowed down her cheeks. "This child was definitely meant to be ours," she told her husband with passion and certainly.

On the little feet of the tiny Chinese child were the shoes she had donated at the church clothing drive so many months before. She recognized the shoes immediately, but just to be positive she looked for the name written on the inside.

When her son was in kindergarten, the teacher had asked the mothers to label all their children's belongings and articles of clothing in case they got lost.

The name of her biological son was still etched there in permanent ink.

The shoes had made their way to their new son before she and her husband had, and it seemed that they would further ease his transition into their home. For as he stepped over the threshold with those little shoes on his tiny feet, his hands would be held by parents convinced that this child was chosen to be theirs.

The long journey to his new parents' heart had already begun.

He was following in his brother's footsteps, all the way home.

~ *Katrina M. Ratz*

THE DINETTE SET

The dinette set was in a sorry state of disrepair. Pressed into service by my children as props for games like musical chairs and Fort Apache, it was badly battered—a mere shadow of the gleaming chrome set that had once graced our kitchen. Stuffing was spilling out of the seat cushions. It had become a real eyesore, and I felt embarrassed each time a visitor entered my home.

In February 1996, I came into a little money and decided to splurge on a new dinette set. I scouted the neighborhood stores that had been recommended by savvy friends, and finally found a set that made my heart sing. I fell in love with its smooth, sleek, contemporary look; the clean, sharp angles of its matching chairs; and its black-and-white Formica finish. For me, buying a dinette set was a special event, and I felt thrilled that I had encountered one that I liked so much. I was, however, less than thrilled to learn its price tag: $680, more than the budget I had allotted in my head. "You have great taste!" the store owner congratulated me. "You've chosen one of the most popular models we sell."

I sighed. Story of my life: champagne taste on a beer budget! I really didn't want to spend that much money, but this set really tempted me. I stood undecided in the store, until finally the practical side of me took charge, and I regretfully told the store owner, "Sorry, but I just can't spend that much. Thanks again."

As I departed the store, I threw one final, yearning look at the dinette set of my dreams.

The next week, I called a friend renowned for her extraordinary bargain-hunting abilities, and she gave me a list of dinette outlets in the neighborhood that sold cheaper models. Armed with the list, I left my home to make the rounds once again.

The day dawned gray and overcast—the kind of day that invariably makes your spirits sag and diminishes your enthusiasm, even for bargain hunting. Nonetheless, I was determined to follow my agenda, so I drove to the first outlet store on my list. Somehow, my friend had made a mistake: All the sets there were priced well over a thousand dollars, and mumbling embarrassed thanks to the store owner, I beat a hasty retreat. By this time it was raining hard, and I ran to my car, parked a block away.

It was then that I saw her. An elderly woman, shuffling slowly in the torrential downpour, clad only in a thin cotton dress and sneakers, with no umbrella, raincoat, or rain hat to protect her from the slashing rain. She looked pale, wan, and vulnerable. She also looked vaguely familiar, and I broke off my wild dash to the car to approach her. As I advanced closer, I made the connection: She was an impoverished woman who made annual visits to the dress shop I owned, sent by a charitable organization to receive clothing donations. (I had an agreement with this organization whereby I gave, through their referral, free clothing to the neighborhood's poor.) She came regularly, once a year, to be outfitted, but I had never seen her outside the store before.

"Linda," I asked in concern, "why are you out on a morning like this?" She began to sob. "Let me drive you to your destination," I said, propelling her to my car.

"What's the matter?" I asked inside the car, as she began to wail in an almost unearthly manner. She poured out her tale of woe, and I felt stricken by her story. She had a daughter who was mentally disabled and married to a mentally disabled man. They had been able to carve out a happy life for themselves and had two normal children. Unfortunately, however, due to their disabilities, they were unable to make a living to sustain their modest lifestyle. Here and there they got odd jobs, and some minimal government assistance, but not enough to live on. The husband's parents were dead, and Linda herself was on welfare. Unable to pay the rent, her daughter had received an eviction notice, and her daughter's landlord had warned her that if he didn't receive the overdue amount by today, she and her family would be ejected from the premises with nowhere to go.

I had three crisp hundred-dollar bills in my wallet. As Linda cried pitifully in my car, I pulled out one of the bills and handed it to her. She stared at the bill in astonishment, kissed me and thanked me effusively, but continued to cry. I paused for a moment, then pulled out a second hundred-dollar bill and handed it to her. She acknowledged her fervent gratitude a second time, but her tears still flowed unabated. I hesitated the third time but thought, "Aw, what the heck? What's a dinette set compared to the eviction of a family?" and handed her the final hundred-dollar bill. Then I drove her to the office of the charitable organization from which she hoped to solicit further help and kissed her good-bye.

As I drove away, I was in a positive frame of mind, confident that I had done the right thing. I was proud that I had made the sacrifice. But as I neared my destination—the second dinette outlet store on my list—I began to waver, assaulted by conflicting emotions. Maybe I was a fool, a patsy, an easy touch. Maybe I should have just given her a hundred? Maybe the charitable organization—funded by individuals certainly wealthier than I—could have undertaken the full cost of the rent, and my sacrifice had been needless. By the time I reached the dinette store, I was no longer sure that my three-hundred-dollar donation had been necessary or even justified.

But as soon as I entered the dinette store, my anxiety about the money dissipated, as my attention was drawn to the dinette set of my dreams—the exact same set I had fallen in love with the week before—standing in the center of the showroom. "Excuse me," I excitedly asked the salesman who approached me, "how much is that set over there—the white one with the black Formica trim?"

"Oh, that one!" he said. "You sure have great taste—it's beautiful, isn't it?"

"So how much is it?" I asked with mounting excitement. "Well," he said slowly, "it really is an expensive set, but you know . . . it's going to be discontinued soon so I don't mind giving you the floor sample. It's ordinarily much more money, but I'll give it to you for . . . three hundred eighty dollars!"

Exactly three hundred dollars less than the original set I had seen the week before.

For a fraction of a second, I closed my eyes to thank God for his blessing on my charity and also . . . for the dinette set!

~ *Yitta Halberstam*

THE PERFECT MATCH

"We're a very ordinary family," insists Suri Granek of Jerusalem, Israel. "The only difference between my family and others is that my children were not borne by me, but rather, for me. They were clearly meant to be ours. We really never needed proof that this was true, but an event that happened five years ago certainly validated our conviction that whoever came our way was destined to be part of our clan."

Despite her modest disclaimer, Suri's family—and its unusual composition—is extraordinary by most people's standards. And the event to which she refers was so singular and uncommon that it made national headlines in Israel.

The saga begins twenty-seven years ago when Seymour Granek and Suri Fogel were married in New York City. "Throughout our engagement and the early years of our marriage," Suri remembers, "we talked about our mutual longing for a large family and agreed that the faster we got started on this enterprise, the better. Maybe it was already considered an unfashionable ambition for women of the 1970s, but all I really wanted was the white picket fence and a warm, noisy, lively brood of kids. "

Yet years passed, and the Graneks remained childless. Comprehensive examinations, painful procedures, myriad infertility treatments—all proved frustratingly fruitless. The legion of doctors whom the Graneks consulted remained clueless;

none could determine the nature of the problem or even find anything wrong. Suri was ovulating normally and had a regular menstrual cycle; each doctor she saw promised that she would eventually get pregnant on her own. But she didn't.

"We waited for seven years before adopting," Suri recalls, "because every single doctor we saw was so positive that I would eventually conceive. We finally turned to the Louise Wise Agency in Manhattan, where we lived. Unlike so many other adoptive parents, who report tales of tribulation in the adoption process, ours went rather smoothly. We were blessed with a three-month-old, blonde-haired, blue-eyed cherub, whom we symbolically named Chaim (life) Simcha (joy). We felt that we would be able to give him a new life and that he in turn would bring us joy. The minute Chaim Simcha was placed in our arms, we knew: No matter how he had come to us, he was ours."

The Graneks adored their new child and relished the joys of parenting. After Chaim Simcha joined their family in November 1979, they reconsidered their earlier dreams. Maybe they couldn't have a large biological family—but what was to stop them from having a huge adoptive one instead?

Once again they turned to Louise Wise, but this time there was a long waiting list at the agency, and social workers gently pointed out that it would be unfair for the Graneks to adopt a second child when so many anxious couples were still waiting for their first.

"If you really want to adopt a second child, suggested one social worker, "why don't you consider a foreign-born child, or go abroad, for that matter?"

The Graneks were put in touch with a placement lawyer in Mexico. They started filing paperwork with both a Mexican adoption agency and the Immigration and Naturalization Service and were advised that the process would take at least six months.

"Astonishingly, it was only two months later [February 1982]," Suri recalls, "that we got a call from Mexico informing us that two babies were suddenly available . . . and each had to be picked up immediately.

"Christina,*a middle-aged woman who had applied to the same Mexican agency, flew with us from New York on the same plane, bound for the same emotional destination—a baby she could soon call her own.

"At the agency, we found the lawyer waiting, a baby cradled in each arm. He handed one baby to Christina, another to me.

"'How did you decide which baby would be ours and which would be Christina's?' I asked, curious to know what criteria had influenced his choice.

"'Oh, it didn't make any difference to me which baby I gave to whom,' he said blithely. 'It was random, really. Call it whimsy, impulse, arbitrary, whatever you like. Nothing specific guided my decision.'"

But when the Graneks glanced casually at the baby's birth certificate, they were shocked to discover that his birth date—September 23—coincided with Suri's own. They were both born on the exact same date! Could it be that this particular baby was destined to be theirs and the lawyer's decision had

* The name Christina is a pseudonym.

not been arbitrary, after all? They named their dark-eyed, five-month-old Mexican baby Baruch after a deceased great-uncle and added the name Matisyahu, which means "gift from God." For that's what Baruch was . . .

The third baby to join the growing Granek family, in January 1983, was only five days old and was also of Mexican extraction. Unlike Baruch Matisyahu, however, this baby seemed to have some Native American genes in her as well. She possessed strong Indian features, straight black hair, and dark skin. She was named Ahuva Leba, Hebrew for "love." The Graneks had it in abundance!

The rapidly expanding Granek family moved to Israel in September 1983, and there they adopted four-month-old Nava Yosefa, a Sabra (Israeli native) of Ethiopian extraction in July 1986, and Ariella Tzvia, a four-year-old Sabra in June 1989.

"Of all my children, it was always Baruch who was the healthiest and most active," muses Suri. "He was president of the student body of his school, a steady volunteer at the Jewish Institute for the Blind, and a star athlete. He excelled in all forms of sports. So it was ironic that of my five children, it was Baruch who became sick.

"In 1995, a few short months after his bar mitzvah, Baruch began complaining of severe leg cramps that were very painful and disrupted his sleep.

"I took him to the local doctor, who checked him out thoroughly but could find nothing wrong. He suspected 'growing pains' but told us to come back if the pains intensified. 'Don't worry,' he said!"

Over time, however, the severity and frequency of the cramps increased. The second visit to the doctor netted tests and a referral to an excellent hospital in Jerusalem, where more tests were run. It was there that the grim diagnosis was handed down by the nephrologist.

"Baruch's kidney function is about 10 percent right now. His potassium levels are sky high. It's probably premature for me to say this, but I think that further analysis will reveal what I've already unhappily concluded: Baruch is suffering from chronic and irreversible kidney disease."

The doctor's suspicions were, sadly, well founded. Not just one, but both of Baruch's kidneys were severely damaged. Physicians treated his condition with several different medications, monitored him constantly, and took his blood pressure several times a day. "You can anticipate his condition being stable for at least a year before he experiences a decline," they told the Graneks.

But they were wrong.

Within only a few short weeks, Baruch had deteriorated rapidly, far in advance of the doctors' timetable. He had become severely anemic, weak, and infirm, and was too frail even to leave his bed. What had become of the strong, healthy, athletic boy Baruch was just a few weeks before? Suri wondered. He had vanished, and a pale wisp of a boy had taken his place.

Two months after the original diagnosis, Baruch had the first of an ongoing series of operations, procedures that initially helped but later failed him, each and every time.

Over a short period of time, the once-robust Baruch had become skeletal, an unrecognizable shadow of his former self. Different methods, multitudinous surgical procedures—including several insertions of temporary and emergency shunts—were attempted time and time again, but each was beset by complications. Finally, the doctor used the word that had hovered in the family's thoughts for so long . . . the word that simultaneously held promise and hope . . . the word that no one had dared breathe, for its enormity was too much to contemplate . . . the word "transplant."

"I want to give Baruch my kidney," Suri told the doctor. "Let me be the first one to be tested as a possible match," she begged.

The doctor stared at Suri. He was familiar with the unusual composition of her family and knew that Baruch was adopted.

What were the chances of Suri—an American of European descent—being a match for a Mexican?

"Forget about it," the doctor advised. "The odds are strong against any pair that is not genetically or ethnically linked in some significant way."

But Suri was not to be dissuaded. If anything, she was known to be a persistent type who believed in following her heart's journey. The unusual family she and Seymour had assembled and loved fervently was certainly testimony to that.

"You'd be wasting your time to even get tested," the doctor said. "Suri," he lectured her, "let me tell you what odds you're facing. You need to fulfill three criteria in order to be considered a viable kidney donor. First, your blood type has to be compatible with the recipient's; second, you must share common antigens; and third, the recipient can't have antibodies that would reject the donor's kidneys. As an adoptive mother, your chances are about nil."

"Let me at least test to see what blood type I am," Suri said stubbornly.

At the lab, the technician glanced sympathetically at Suri as she gave her the news. "I know you're testing for compatibility with your son," she said compassionately. "I am sorry to tell you that you have a rare blood type—B positive—which only 8 percent of the world's population has. I know how depressing the news must be."

But Suri was, much to the technician's surprise, elated instead. "This is the best news!" she shouted jubilantly. "Baruch is also Type B positive!"

Heartened by the wonderful coincidence, Suri then bombarded the doctor with pleas to be tissue-typed—the test where compatibility between donor and recipient almost always resides in their sharing a common genetic heritage.

It was not that the doctor wasn't supportive or understanding of Suri's enormous drive to give the gift of life to her son. It was precisely because he was so sensitive to the pain and trauma that Suri had undergone that he did not want her to suffer any further. He wanted to spare her the disappointment of not being able to literally give of herself to her son.

"Listen," he told Suri, "it's quite a surprise that you and Baruch share the same blood type, but the statistics indicate that 8 percent of the population do. But statistics also reveal that your chances of sharing common antigens are about zero. The whole thing's impossible."

"It doesn't hurt to try," Suri reasoned. The doctor threw up his hands in surrender, and she proceeded with the tissue-typing test.

Waiting at the nephrologist's office several weeks later for the test results to come in finally, Suri paced the floor nervously. Every minute seemed like an hour, every hour an eternity, as she felt her son's life hang in the balance. Then the phone rang, and she overhead the following conversation between two secretaries on the speakerphone.

"Great news, they have half of their antigens in common," the lab secretary reported to the nephrologist's assistant, who sat stunned in her seat.

"I'm shocked!" she told her colleague over the phone.

"Why are you so shocked?" the lab secretary asked, puzzled. "After all, she's his mother, isn't she?"

"You don't understand," the nephrologist's secretary responded. "She's his adoptive mother. She's an American Jew of European descent. He's a Mexican American. They share no common genetic link."

Baruch's antibodies also proved compatible with Suri's. So, on all three counts—blood type, shared antigens, and compatible antibodies—adoptive mother and adoptive son were a perfect match!

But Baruch didn't want to take his mother's kidney. He felt that it was too great a sacrifice. He had heard that kidney transplants are exceedingly painful procedures, especially for the donor.

"It's going to hurt you!" he protested to Suri.

"Baruch," Suri replied, "the emotional pain of watching you suffer is far greater than any physical pain I would ever have to endure."

The successful transplant took place exactly nine months after the original diagnosis. Suri feels that the number is laden with meaning.

"Baruch was a brand-new person immediately after the transplant," she says. "I felt as if he had been reborn."

The date of the transplant also held special significance for her. "The transplant took place on the [Hebrew date] eighteenth of Tishrei," she remembers. In Hebrew, eighteen symbolizes *chai*—life.

Baruch is now eighteen years old, has just graduated from high school, and, as a result of his medical history, plans to become a doctor so that he may help others as he was helped.

"Today," Suri says proudly, "Baruch is healthy, muscular, physically fit, and, altogether, doing beautifully. Although he has had to give up his beloved soccer because the kidney was transplanted in his abdomen (a vulnerable place for soccer players), he continues to shine as a basketball star."

Suri recalls with wonder the day the Mexican lawyer placed the infant Baruch in her arms, his action seemingly dictated by sheer whim.

What if he had been placed in Christina's arms instead? What were the chances that Christina would also be a compatible donor? Would Baruch even be alive today if Christina had been arbitrarily chosen as his adoptive mother, and not Suri?

Suri is awestruck by the miracle of their perfect match, but modestly discounts her own role in literally saving Baruch's life.

"These are my children," she says simply. "The only difference is that they didn't grow inside of me. They grew inside my heart, instead."

~ *Suri Granek, as told to the authors*

A DRIVE TO AKRON

everal decades ago, Lillian was an energetic, spirited, fearless young woman who loved driving long distances, did not tire easily, and relished any opportunity to do a good deed. This unusual combination of characteristics meant that she was frequently asked to perform favors for people.

Because of her good-naturedness, she was enlisted to drive two young servicemen to Fort Sill, Oklahoma, from her hometown in Pennsylvania. Having faithfully fulfilled her mission and dropped the men on base, she turned her car around and immediately started back home. Heading down the highway, though, Lillian had second thoughts.

"Now, you're not being very realistic," she chastised herself. "You have a good eighteen-hour trip ahead of you. Better fill up on some coffee first."

She spotted a little diner off the highway, ablaze with light. She pulled in. Grabbing her thermos from the car, she went inside and asked the waitress to fill it to the top. She also ordered a separate cup to sip while she sat waiting at the counter. She was drinking her coffee, lost in thought, when a plaintive voice broke her reverie.

A few seats down from her, a young serviceman in uniform sat quietly weeping. A waitress hovered over him, anxiously trying to soothe him with words of comfort, but nothing she said seemed to help. Lillian listened intently.

"It's my first child, and I want to be there for my wife," he said. "I can't believe I'm going to miss the birth of my baby!"

"Are you sure it's not false labor?" the waitress asked.

"She just called from the hospital. The doctor is sure she's in the early stages of labor. It might be a while, he says, since it's the first, but the baby is definitely on its way."

"I can't believe you have no way to get home," the waitress said sympathetically.

"There is no plane service from here to Akron, and the next bus and train out don't leave until tomorrow. . . . Tomorrow will probably be too late!"

"Excuse me," Lillian said. She stood up and approached the serviceman. "I'm sorry, but I couldn't help but overhear your conversation. Did you say that you have to get to Akron, as in Akron, Ohio?"

"That's right," he said. He looked up at her in puzzlement, wondering where she was going with this.

"Well, this is a mighty interesting coincidence . . . ," she said, smiling. "I'm headed toward Pennsylvania, which is about an hour and a half away from Akron. I can drive you there, and then you can try to get a hitch from there to Akron. I'll be glad to give you a lift."

"This is unbelievable!" the serviceman exclaimed. "You are so kind. Please . . . let me pay you for the trip."

"Oh, absolutely not," Lillian said. "I'm driving there anyway. I'm glad to help you out. Hop in."

All through the trip, the serviceman kept reiterating his joy, his gratitude, his appreciation, his insistence that Lillian allow him to pay for the gas, the tolls, the trip itself—but Lillian was more obstinate than he.

"Save your money for the baby," she advised. "I told you . . . I was heading in that direction anyway."

But when they reached Lillian's hometown and she turned around to tell the serviceman—who had stretched out on the back seat to catch a few winks—that they had arrived, her expression softened. He was fast asleep, and he looked so young and vulnerable and sweet. His first baby, he had said. What if he couldn't find a hitch to Akron, after all? Having come such a long way, how would he feel if he missed the momentous event of his baby's birth?

In a split second, she decided. She wouldn't wake the serviceman. She would extend herself and drive him all the way to the hospital in Akron. "For me," she reasoned, "it's just three hours out of my way. For him, it's a lifetime."

When they reached Akron, Lillian gently roused him and told him where they were. Startled, he gazed at her, overwhelmed by her kindness. "You've really gone out on a limb for me," he said. "How can I ever repay you? Please give me your name and address, so I can send you something as a token of my appreciation."

But Lillian was a stubborn sort.

"You'll do no such thing," she commanded him sternly. "You'll need every penny you have for all your baby's needs, wait and see. . . . I'm delighted I was able to help you out, and good luck to you. Bye." Lillian waved one final time and quickly drove away.

But not back home, after all. She faced another hour-and-a-half trip, and even the tireless Lillian had finally become weary and spent. It was three o'clock in the morning, and what she needed more than anything else right now was . . . a bed.

"I know!" she decided spontaneously. "I'll go to Dot's and sleep there."

Dot, her sister, lived in a trailer park about ten miles from Akron. Even though it was the middle of the night, she knew she was welcome at her sister's anytime. Her sister would throw open the door, smile at her warmly, and excitedly usher her inside.

But when she arrived at the trailer and pounded insistently at the door, no one answered. "That's strange," Lillian muttered. "Dot's not a heavy sleeper . . ."

She went around to the bedroom window and hammered on it loudly. She waited expectantly for the figure of her sister to peer out the window or be framed in the kitchen doorway. Or, if not her sister, then at least her grandmother, or her niece . . . But no one, not a single member of the family, stirred at all.

Lillian ran back to the trailer door and knocked noisily once more. Still no response from inside. But she had managed to awaken the next-door neighbor. "Is something wrong?" he called out to her as he emerged from his trailer, clad only in pajamas.

It was then that she smelled gas.

She motioned to him wildly. "I think something's the matter with my sister and her family. . . . I can't wake them up, and I think I smell gas. . . . Could you come here and tell me if you smell it too?"

The neighbor ran over and sniffed. "Smells like gas to me," he said, alarmed. "Let me get some tools from my car."

He raced back and pried open Dorothy's trailer door with a tire iron. As the two entered, they were engulfed by heavy gas fumes and began choking. Lillian found the limp, dazed figures of her family members strewn around the bedrooms, and she and the neighbor pulled them out of the trailer into the brisk fresh air. Thankfully, every single one of them survived.

Decades later, Lillian still feels touched by grace; the episode remains one of the defining moments of her life.

"If I hadn't picked up the serviceman in Oklahoma and driven him all the way to Akron, my family might very well have died that night. Sometimes, when you're performing an act of kindness, the person who ends up benefiting the most is yourself!"

~ *Lillian Miller*

THE SAME DREAM

*J*ody Robbins* didn't believe in the prophetic power of dreams, but this particular one had been vivid and disturbing.

She shivered when the dream roused her from her sleep in the middle of the night. She had seen her elderly mother's home engulfed in flames, and, in the dream, her mother was burned beyond recognition.

The clock at her bedside announced that it was three in the morning, and as much as Jody wanted to call her mother at that very moment and be reassured by the sound of her comforting voice, she also didn't want to stress her already fragile heart. So Jody promised herself that she would call her mother first thing in the morning and tell her about the ominous dream.

But when she called, her mother—independent, self-sufficient, and a skeptic to boot—only laughed. She was more psychologically than psychically oriented, and she scolded Jody in a bantering voice, "So is this then your secret wish . . . that I die?"

Jody wasn't offended; she knew it was her mother's feeble attempt to disarm her, to diminish her concern. But she couldn't be swayed from her conviction that the dream had been portentous; it was too powerful to shrug off so lightly.

"Mom!" she began to plead in protest, when suddenly she heard a familiar click on the line.

* The names in this story are pseudonyms.

"Oh, there goes that darned call waiting again," her mother sighed. "Am I ever sorry that I signed up for that service from the phone company! All my calls keep getting interrupted, and I always end up insulting somebody. Hold on a minute, dear, while I take that call, and I'll be right back."

Her mother hated keeping people waiting, so Jody was surprised when several minutes elapsed and her mother still had not returned to her call.

That's strange, she thought. Mom never keeps me waiting so long. She was about to hang up when her mother's voice—now breathless—came back on the line.

"Oh, Jody," she apologized. "I'm so sorry. That was your sister Carol, calling from Hawaii, where you know she's been vacationing . . ."

"Mom, didn't you tell me that Carol called you yesterday? Is everything okay with her? I mean, it's not like her to make so many long-distance calls!"

"Well, Jody, actually, Carol's call unnerved me just a little. . . . It's so strange," her mother laughed nervously, "but it seems that last night, Carol had the exact same dream you had."

"Mom!" Jody shrieked. "What did she dream exactly?"

"Jody, it's no use going over it. . . . Your dreams weren't similar. They were identical."

"Well, then, Mom, that does it. No ifs, buts, or maybes. I want you to move in with me for a few days, and we'll get some professionals to inspect your house to make sure there are no fire traps or anything to beware of."

"Jody!" her mother said sharply. "That's ridiculous; you know I need my space and . . . I don't believe in dreams."

"Even when two sisters—halfway across the world from each other—have the exact same dream on the exact same night? It gives me goose bumps, Mom. If you don't want to do it for yourself, please do it for me."

Over her loud, strenuous objections, Jody drove a small van to her mother's house, packed two suitcases with clothes and her mother's most precious possessions, and said firmly, "You're staying with me."

The following night, a gas explosion erupted in Jody's mother's house, incinerating the house in a matter of minutes.

The house was destroyed, but Jody's mother was out of harm's way, thanks to her daughters' twin dreams.

At the time of the fire, she was safely ensconced in her daughter's home.

~ *Judith Leventhal*

BLESSINGS

*I*t was December 23. My children and I lived in a tiny house. Being a single mom, going to college, and supporting my children completely alone, Christmas looked bleak. As I looked around me, realization dawned with a slow, twisting pain. We were poor.

Our tiny house had two bedrooms, both off the living room. They were so small that my baby daughter's crib barely fit into one, and my son's twin bed and dresser into the other. There was no way they could share a room, so I made my bed every night on the living room floor. The three of us shared the only closet in the house. We were snug, always only a few feet from each other, day and night. With no doors on the children's rooms, I could see and hear them at all times. It made them feel secure and made me feel close to them—a benefit I would not have had in other circumstances.

It was late, almost eleven. The snow was falling softly, silently. I was wrapped in a blanket, sitting at the window watching the powdery flakes flutter in the moonlight, when my front door vibrated against a pounding fist. Alarmed, I wondered who would be at my home so late on a snowy winter night. I opened the door to find several strangers grinning from ear to ear, their arms laden with boxes and bags. Confused, but finding their joyous spirit contagious, I grinned right back.

"Are you Susan?" The man stepped forward as he sort of pushed a box at me.

Nodding stupidly, unable to find my voice, I was sure they thought I was mentally deficient.

"These are for you." The woman thrust another box at me with a huge, beaming smile. The porch light and the snow falling behind her cast a glow on her dark hair, lending her an angelic appearance. I looked down into her box. It was filled with treats, a fat turkey, and all the makings of a traditional Christmas dinner. My eyes filled with tears as the realization of what they were there for washed over me.

Finally coming to my senses, I invited them in. Following the husband were two children, staggering with the weight of their gifts for my little family. This wonderful, beautiful family, who were total strangers to me, somehow knew exactly what we needed. They brought wrapped gifts for each of us, a full buffet for me to make on Christmas, and many "extras" that I could never afford. Visions of a beautiful, "normal" Christmas literally danced in my head. Somehow my secret wish for Christmas was materializing right in front of me.

My mysterious angels then handed me an envelope, giving me another round of grins, and each of them hugged me. They wished me a Merry Christmas and disappeared into the night as suddenly as they had appeared. The whole experience seemed to have lasted for hours, yet it was over in less than a couple of minutes.

Amazed and deeply touched, I looked around me at the boxes and gifts strewn at my feet and felt the ache of depression suddenly being transformed into a childlike joy. I began to cry. I cried hard, sobbing tears of the deepest gratitude. A great sense of peace filled me. The knowledge of God's love reaching into my tiny corner of the world enveloped me like a warm quilt. My heart was full. I dropped to my knees amid all the boxes and offered a heartfelt prayer of thanks.

Suddenly I remembered the envelope. Like a child I ripped it open and gasped at what I saw. A shower of bills flitted to the floor. Gathering them up, I began to count the five-, ten-, and twenty-dollar bills. My vision blurred with tears. I counted the money, then counted it again to make sure I had it right. Now sobbing, I said it out loud. "One hundred dollars."

There was no way the visitors could have known it, but I had just received a disconnect notice from the gas company. I simply didn't have the money needed and feared my family would be without heat by Christmas. The envelope of cash would give us warmth and a tree for Christmas. Suddenly, we had all we needed and more.

It is now several years since our Christmas angels visited. I have since remarried, and we are happy and richly blessed. Every year since that Christmas in 1993, we have chosen a family less blessed than we are. We bring them carefully selected gifts, food, and treats, and as much money as we can spare. It's our way of passing on what was given to us. It is the "ripple effect" in motion. We hope that the cycle continues and that some day, the families that we share with will also pass it on.

~ *Susan Fahncke*

PAID FORWARD

*M*y husband is the ultimate Good Samaritan. Wherever he goes, wherever he happens to be, he's always performing random acts of kindness, often for people he doesn't know, and sometimes for people he doesn't even see. Most of the time I am proud and gratified to be married to such a man, but once in a while I get annoyed when I think he's being excessive. When this spirit moves me (on rare occasions I must admit) I start to sulk, fume, and—if what he's done really strikes me as extravagant—boil over with rage. "Hmmph," I'll sputter indignantly, "this is all very nice, but when was the last time somebody did something like this for you or for me? Are you the only Good Samaritan left in town?"

But last week these doubts were given short shrift by a universe far wiser than I.

My husband and I were idly window-shopping one day in a local business district where cars were parked along the curb next to meters. Suddenly, we noticed a grim-faced meter maid stomping determinedly down the street, studying each meter intently, pen poised, prepared to write tickets. My husband immediately pulled out all the change in his pockets and began running down the street, frantically inserting quarters into all the expired meters, preempting the meter maid.

When she finally advanced upon him, it was with raised eyebrows and a scowling face; he in turn flashed her a triumphant grin and a roguish wink. From a distance, I watched my husband tenderly. It struck me that he was engaging in the highest form of charity: None of the people whose cars he had saved from being ticketed would ever know their benefactor; they probably wouldn't even know they had one! I was proud of him, to be sure. Still, when he returned from his labors, that little, cynical voice that I contend with all the time had the final word: "That was beautiful, honey . . . but when was the last time somebody did that for you or for me?"

The next day, I was shopping again, this time in a different business district, and parked my car next to a meter. In a dress shop filled with luscious creations, I lost all sense of time, and when I glanced down at my watch, I realized with a start that my time on the meter must have expired. I hurried out of the store and ran toward my car, parked a block away. With a sinking heart, I saw a meter maid advancing toward the car.

Now, my husband, a perfectly reasonable man in all other respects, gets totally enraged when I get a parking ticket. He considers it the height of irresponsibility and a horrible waste of money besides. A parking ticket means at least three hours of serious fighting, followed by a full day of shameful recriminations and mournful head-shaking. I have learned (painfully) to avoid getting parking tickets, at all costs.

But when I saw the meter maid just a few feet away from my car, I knew all hope was lost. There was no way I could get to the meter before she did. I almost wept in consternation.

Suddenly, I saw an unfamiliar-looking man sprint across the street, dash over to my meter, and insert a quarter. At that point the meter maid approached, and he smiled broadly at her. Then he turned and strode quickly down the street. I rushed after him to thank him, wondering, "Who could it be? Is it someone who knows me . . . maybe a neighbor, a relative . . . someone who recognized the car and wanted to help me out?" But when I caught up with him and called to him to stop, it was a complete stranger who turned around.

"You just rescued me from the meter maid!" I bubbled. "Thank you so much—I can't believe you did that! Do you know my husband by any chance, and did you recognize our car? What made you do it?"

"Oh, I don't know your husband, and I don't know your car," he said. "But I happened to see the meter maid coming, and I thought, what a shame—she's going to ticket that car. All it cost me was twenty-five cents to save you from a twenty-five-dollar ticket."

I was overwhelmed, and I couldn't thank the man enough. "Oh, it's OK really," he said. "I do this all the time!"

~ *Yitta Halberstam*

A WONDERFUL MOMENT

I was excited to meet Sandi. My editor had said we were kindred spirits, and from the moment we started to correspond, we both knew that she was right. Sandi was a graphic artist and calligrapher. Her work was bright, colorful, and playful, especially her well-known "trademark"—a little angel named Ariane whom she drew and put on bookmarks. She liked to present these bookmarks to people as little gifts, usually with the saying "Miracles happen to those who believe!" inscribed below the drawing. A woman after my own heart!

Sandi and I wanted to meet in person, but it seemed impossible, since I live in North Dakota and she in Massachusetts. On a whim, I wrote to tell her that my family and I would be vacationing on Martha's Vineyard in July, and I had one day when I knew I would be free. Curiously, she said that she was going to be visiting her parents on Cape Cod that very same day. I offered to ferry over from the island, and she asked if her mother could join us for the fun of it.

In spite of the warmth of our previous exchanges, I admit that I was nervous about meeting someone who was basically still a stranger. Although the sound of the ferry engine and the rhythm of the sea usually calm me, I found myself reaching in my book bag for a small volume I had brought with me, *Peace Is Every Step* by the Vietnamese Zen Buddhist monk Thich Nhat Hanh. The book was little known by others, but well loved by me. It contained a meditation that I found very soothing: "Breathing in, I calm my body. Breathing out, I smile. Dwelling in the present moment, I know this is a wonderful moment." I closed my eyes, reciting it over and over as the ferry cut through the sound.

Sandi and her mother turned out to be delightful, and the afternoon started to slip away more quickly than any of us wanted it to. I felt comfortable with both of them, and judging from their smiles and enthusiasm, they felt the same about me.

"I have to admit something," Sandi said gently. "I was both excited and nervous about meeting you, so on my way over here, I was reading this wonderful little book called *Peace Is Every Step*. It has this one breathing exercise I really like." She recited just the one I had used during the ferry ride.

My jaw must have dropped, because they both looked at me with alarmed faces and said "What's wrong?" simultaneously.

I silently reached in my book bag and showed them my book. They gasped.

From the first letter, Sandi and I had sensed that we would be friends. From that moment on, we knew we were soul mates, too.

~ *Robin L. Silverman*

THE UNLUCKY THIEF

*W*as it bad timing, bad luck, or something else? Colleen didn't even know that her checkbook had been stolen until she was handed one of her checks—with a forged signature—to cash.

Out of the dozens of banks in the city, the brazen thief had made the fatal mistake of trying to cash the stolen check at the very institution where the rightful owner worked—as a teller.

And it was precisely this teller's window that the perpetrator randomly approached to make the transaction.

Hey, this is my check! Colleen thought, her eyes widening in disbelief, as she noted her own name and address printed at the top. She had recently ordered new checks, and now, it seemed, one of them had somehow come into the possession of the very woman standing in front of her . . . face to face!

Thinking quickly, Colleen tried to stall the thief while she motioned quietly to a coworker nearby. The coworker alerted a bank security officer and simultaneously put in a call to the police.

While she waited for the police to arrive, Colleen kept making small talk.

"So . . . where'd you get the check?" she asked the thief casually.

The thief told her that a woman had given it to her so that she could buy some clothes. "The woman is right outside . . . do you want to talk to her?" the thief asked, apparently growing nervous.

"Yes, I would."

The thief wheeled around and walked out the door. She didn't come back.

Although some of the bank staff followed, the woman was faster on her feet than they, and she disappeared in a flash.

But a security guard working for a neighboring company heard the commotion, spotted the woman, and joined in the chase. As the thief ducked into an alleyway, she hurled a pad of personal checks into the street. She was then wrestled to the ground by the security officer and two other men and held until the police arrived.

In reconstructing the robbery, police concluded that the new checkbooks had been delivered to Colleen's house earlier that morning, when she was already on her way to work. Because the box of checks would not fit into the mail slot, the mail carrier had left the package outside Colleen's door, making it an easy target for thieves to snatch. The odds that the thief would show up at that particular bank were amazing. Colleen usually rotated between different branches of the bank and just happened to be working at that branch that particular day.

Colleen had just come on duty a few minutes before the thief walked in the door.

~ *Judith Leventhal*

A RIDE IN THE NICK OF TIME

I'm getting more and more absentminded by the day, I berated myself, as I struggled to find the change I needed to buy a subway token for my trip home.

It was true. As I advanced headlong into middle age, my forgetfulness was becoming increasingly more pronounced, precipitating all kinds of little crises and minor disasters.

How did I manage to travel to Manhattan without my wallet in my purse? I wondered. Had I found spare change at the bottom of my bag to buy my subway token in Brooklyn? Well, if I had, there wasn't any left. Bad news: With no wallet in my purse and with no welcome jangle of loose coins coming from deep inside, I found myself vacillating between laughter and despair. Imagine, a middle-class woman from a comfortable home who lacks $1.50 to get back home!

It wasn't a tragedy or an emergency, but in that moment I felt vulnerable and lost. I didn't travel to Manhattan often and didn't know my way around the city. I had no friends or acquaintances in the vicinity and couldn't think of anyone who worked in the surrounding area. So what was I to do?

I hunted again in my purse, hoping that I had somehow overlooked a nook or cranny where that seemingly insignificant but all-important sum might hide. Oh, to have $1.50 in my hand! I looked wistfully at the commuters rushing by, longing for a familiar face to suddenly appear. I felt invisible and helpless as people whizzed by without giving me so much as a glance. What should I do?

Well, I told myself, you could throw yourself on the mercy of the token booth clerk and beg her to let you through the turnstile.

Or you could find a policeman and ask him for $1.50.

But I couldn't do either of those things. I felt so ashamed. I knew it was irrational—I knew that this could happen to anyone and that there was nothing to be embarrassed about. But still, reasonable or not, I flushed with mortification.

The subway was dank with sour odors, and I needed to come up for oxygen.

Maybe if I go outside, I'll get revived by the fresh air and I'll be able to think more clearly. Or better yet, maybe I'll find the money I need obligingly dropped on the sidewalk right at the top of the subway steps!

These were the two better-case scenarios I concocted in my head, as I ascended the stairs. But what awaited me outside was better than anything I could possibly have conceived in my wildest imagination.

A yellow taxicab—one of the tens of thousands that rove Manhattan's streets—had just pulled up to the curb and was in the process of discharging a passenger.

My heart leaped when I spotted it, and without a moment's hesitation, I slid into the front seat as soon as the passenger stepped out.

"I can't believe this!" I exclaimed, dizzy with relief. "This is what you call perfect timing. How did you know to be at the corner of Broadway and Forty-Second Street at precisely 5:02 p.m. just as I emerged from the station?"

"God must have sent me," my husband the cabdriver chuckled, as he turned on the "Off Duty" sign indicating the end of his twelve-hour day.

"Home?" he asked.

"Home," I sighed contentedly.

"Always at your service," he said as he swept off his cap in a mocking motion.

"You or God?" I shot back in response.

~ *Claire Halberstam*

THE REUNION

James Williams* was just one of the many stroke patients at the hospital tended to by an array of practitioners, one of whom was nurse's aide Juno Perkins. Juno wished she could be more attentive to each and every individual under her care, but harried and overworked, she usually had little personal time to spend with any of her charges. As she rushed about her chores—emptying bedpans, straightening sheets—she engaged in casual chit-chat, but conversation was limited and rarely meaningful. She knew little about her patients, and they, in turn, knew even less about her.

But one thing she did want them to know, including James Williams, was her name, and he kept on forgetting it. One day, she showed him her hospital identification card to help him remember. As she pointed her name out to him and pronounced it in a loud and clear voice, she was oblivious to the visitor sitting at James's bedside.

"Juno" she articulated slowly. "J-u-n-o."

The visitor—who happened to be James's brother, Todd—registered mild surprise at her unusual name.

"I had a daughter named Juno," he offered casually. "But that was so many years ago . . ."

He didn't think of pursuing the conversation, but Juno on the other hand wouldn't consider dropping it.

* The names in this story, a dramatization, are pseudonyms.

"Did your daughter have a middle name?" she pressed.

"Yes," Todd Williams answered, "a strange name that her mother had insisted upon—Domingo."

It was then that Juno began to cry and understanding first dawned upon Todd.

"Oh my God," he screamed, "I've found my daughter!"

The two had been searching for each other for over forty years. By chance, they had ended up in the same hospital room, caring for James Williams.

"It was miraculous the way we met," said Juno, who hadn't seen her father since she was seven years old.

Todd Williams had separated from his wife in the 1950s, but remained in touch with his two daughters, then six and seven. He visited them regularly and loved them with all his heart.

"But one week I came to their apartment, and they had moved," he remembers sadly. No forwarding address had been left behind. Neighbors said they had no information. Todd's beloved children had vanished, and it was as if they had ceased to exist.

But not in his mind, not in his heart. He scoured the city streets for them, "driving up and down blocks in different Chicago neighborhoods, going to different schools to look for them." Decades later, he was still thumbing his way through the white pages phone book, dialing up dozens of women with the same name as his ex-wife. But unbeknownst to him, she had remarried and had a new surname. His efforts were in vain. "But still . . . I never gave up."

Juno's phone book was also well thumbed. She too had raked its pages for decades, seeking clues to her father's whereabouts. But for her as well, the phone book proved to be a dead end; it yielded no signs, no hints, no trails to her father's home or heart. Williams, after all, is a very common name, so common in fact, that when James Williams became one of her patients, she didn't give his name a second thought.

"What's in a name?" Shakespeare asks in *Romeo and Juliet*. "That which we call a rose / By any other name would smell as sweet."

Shakespeare was wrong. Sometimes a name can change your destiny, shape your life, reunite you with a long-lost father.

What's in a name? Ask Juno Perkins. That's J-u-n-o.

~ *Judith Leventhal*

HERO ON THE TRACKS

As a female deputy sheriff working in Hillsborough County, Florida, I've certainly had my fair share of hair-raising experiences, but one particular episode that occurred six years ago unnerves me to this day.

In 1994, I was working the midnight shift and patrolling an area that was mostly rural. It had been a quiet night, unpunctuated by crises or diversions of any kind, and I was feeling kind of restless. At about two o'clock in the morning, however, I received a call from the police dispatcher. A van was stuck on the railroad tracks approximately seven miles away from my position.

I sped toward the site. Approaching the tracks in my car, I was alarmed to see a train, loaded with phosphates, racing toward the van. It was on an inevitable collision course with the van, and I was the only one who knew the fate that awaited both the oblivious train crew and the passengers inside the stranded vehicle. The enormity of this pressed upon me: Only I possessed this knowledge, and only I had the ability to stop a terrible accident from occurring. The adrenaline coursed through my body.

I radioed my dispatcher and tersely reported that a train was headed toward the van. I knew that the engineer needed a mile's notice to slam down the brakes effectively, and I told the dispatcher to get in touch with him fast. The van was stalled on a curve of the train tracks, and unless he had prior warning, the engineer would never see it until it was too late.

I outraced the train, and when I arrived at the scene, I saw an empty van sitting on the tracks, abandoned by its occupants. I was relieved that the van passengers were no longer in the path of danger, but the train crew still was. If the train hit the van, it would derail for sure. Serious injuries—or even death—could result from such a wreck.

I called my dispatcher again. She said she could not make contact with the train but would keep on trying. My adrenaline pumped.

I tried to park my cruiser and run my emergency lights, but I was stymied. A swamp abutted one side of the tracks, and the other side was fenced in with cattle. I was forced to park almost two hundred feet away and found myself in the yard of the only house in the area.

An elderly gentleman and his young grandson ran out of the house to meet me. It was from this house that the call to the police dispatcher had originally been made. The man had been the one who had sighted the van, and he had also seen a group of teenagers leave the vehicle and flee on foot.

I called the dispatcher again. She still had not been able to establish contact with the crew. Far off in the distance, I could hear the rumble of the train. The quiet country night echoed its whistle.

I tried to push the van off the tracks, but it wouldn't budge an inch. The residents of the house could not be a source of assistance, either. The elderly man was too frail to help me, and his grandson was too young.

I picked up the phone to call the dispatcher again. This time I frantically shouted that it was an emergency! Equally frustrated, the dispatcher yelled back that she hadn't been able to reach the engineer but that she was trying hard.

I could feel the train's vibrations as I stood helpless on the tracks, panic-stricken. Which way do I run? I wondered. Who will find my body? I could see the train's light shining through the trees around the bend.

I felt powerless to halt the inevitable head-on collision. There was nothing left that I could do. I had no choice but to move the three of us—the elderly man, his grandson, and myself—to higher ground and safety. His house adjoined the railroad tracks, and if the crash happened, the train cars might crumple up accordion style in his yard and maybe even smash into his house.

"Is there anyone else in the house?" I yelled.

"My wife, she's sleeping . . ."

"Wake her up fast, and get into my car." I would attempt to race away from the crash site as fast as I could.

It was then, in the early morning darkness, down a dirt frontage road, that a teenage boy in a pickup truck suddenly appeared. Blond, wearing a baseball cap and chewing tobacco, he pulled up alongside me and asked in an easygoing manner, "You need some help, officer?"

"I've got to get that van off the tracks before the train hits it!"

"I've got a tow rope; I'll have it off in a jiffy," he replied calmly, and then gunned his motor as he raced toward the tracks. Apprehensive, I followed on foot and returned to the site

I had just evacuated. I knew that we would both be in mortal danger if he couldn't remove the van fast enough, but I couldn't let him go alone.

Within a matter of thirty seconds he had the van off the tracks, and the whole scenario changed. The collision would be avoided. The train crew would be saved. They would never even know how close to derailment—and death—they had come.

Elated and exhausted at the same time, I made my way back to reassure the elderly man and his grandson, who were still standing in the front yard some twenty-five feet away.

"The van is off the tracks!" I shouted, dizzy with relief.

"And here comes the train now!" the man pointed.

Trembling, we watched as it peacefully whizzed by. We shook our heads in disbelief, shock, and awe. We were overcome by thoughts of the near calamity that had been averted at, literally, the last possible moment.

I turned to the elderly man and his grandson and took their names and other pertinent information for my official police report. Then I thought about the teenage boy, who surely deserved a police commendation for his heroism.

"Now if you'll excuse me," I apologized to the two, "I need to go talk to the boy in the truck who pulled the van off the tracks."

The elderly man looked confused. "What boy?" he asked.

I gestured toward the van that had been towed to the dirt road alongside the railroad tracks. "You know, the young man who used his truck to move the van," I happily reminded him.

"No disrespect, ma'am, but nobody's been down this road but you."

I hurried down to the train tracks and to the van that sat beside it.

The boy, his tow rope, and his truck were gone.

The van remained on the side of the tracks; it had clearly been pulled off. But to this day I do not know who hauled it out of danger's reach that fateful night.

~ *Jennifer Greco*

THE GOOD-BYE

*M*y father was ill in Denver; I lived in New York, where family obligations and small children kept me home, waiting for news. He had cancer, and it was terminal; but the doctor could offer no prognosis. It could be a month, or it could be days, he said.

One night, a dream transported me back to my childhood home in Pittsburgh, where my father had lived the bulk of his life. In the dream, I clearly saw the winding staircase that led from the second floor to the third, and on the flight of stairs my father stood, bathed in an aura of light. The light was unlike anything I had ever seen in this earthly world; it was dazzling, resplendent, and very strong.

My father's back was turned to me as he ascended the staircase slowly. I felt a tremendous sense of loss as I saw him mount the steps; the sensation was poignant and knifed my heart. I wanted to call out to him, but something held me back; I was struck mute. Then suddenly, he turned around, looked directly at me standing at the bottom of the landing, smiled tenderly, and raised his arm in greeting. But it was not hello that he waved with his hand; it was clearly good-bye.

Just then the phone rang and woke me from my dream. It was my sister in Denver informing me that our father had just passed away. She was surprised at my calm response.

I was calm because I felt certain that my father had

appeared in my dream to bid me a final farewell. I was calm because I was confident that his spirit would continue to watch over me long after his body had turned to dust. And I felt calm because I knew, beyond a shadow of a doubt, that he was surely in paradisiacal realms, for I had seen him on the stairway, making his gradual ascent toward heaven.

~ Claire Halberstam

THE REBBE

*T*n 1992, my daughter Sinaya was treated for a certain
medical condition and, as part of her treatment, was given
a very potent drug. It was only a few weeks later that she learned
something that would become for her—simultaneously—both
cause for joy and a source of unremitting horror.

She discovered that, unbeknownst to her, she had been
pregnant when she had ingested the medication and that the
powerful drug was one that was known to cause birth defects.

She and her husband agonized over what to do. This
was their first child. They had originally greeted the news of
the pregnancy with great elation. But now they were seized
with dread and panic at the possible consequences of the
medication. To bring a deformed baby into this world! It was
too cruel.

Their doctor had not been able to give them the assurances
they wanted to hear. It was very possible, he had said, that the
baby would be born perfectly normal. Then again, he had said,
it was possible that the baby might not be normal at all.

After many nights of soul-searching, the couple made their
decision. They would not abort, but would proceed with the
pregnancy.

Still, Sinaya couldn't stop herself from worrying throughout
the pregnancy. Given the reality of the situation, her obsession
was understandable. She was constantly besieged with nightmare

visions of a grossly deformed baby cradled in her arms. As the pregnancy progressed, she became increasingly tense and anxious. My heart ached for my daughter. Her pain was too much to bear. I couldn't take it anymore; I felt I had to do something concrete to obliterate—or at least diminish—her torment.

For many years, I had been told amazing stories about a contemporary Jewish sage/saint known as the Lubavitcher Rebbe. He was an internationally famous Hasidic rabbi who, people said, performed miracles. Although I was not a constituent of his group, nor did I know anyone within his fold, I decided to reach out to him for help.

I faxed a letter to his office, asking for a blessing for my daughter's unborn child. The very next day, I received a phone call from a man who identified himself as the Rebbe's personal secretary. He had a message for me from the Rebbe, he said. The baby was going to be perfectly healthy, normal, and well, and he would grow up to be a fine and wonderful human being.

I was delirious with joy, dizzy with relief. "Rabbi," I asked, "do you promise this is true?"

"The Rebbe promises that everything will be fine. Mazel tov."

That night, Sinaya called me to report that her water had just broken and that she was on her way to the hospital.

"Sinaya," I told her, "don't be afraid of anything. You got a blessing from the Rebbe today, and he promised that everything will be okay."

As I hung up, I glanced at the clock, saw that it was 8 p.m., and was startled to realize an uncanny coincidence. Exactly twenty-five years before, on the exact same date, also at 8 p.m. in the evening, my own water had broken—and later that night, I had given birth to Sinaya!

Sinaya gave birth the next morning to a robust, sturdy, healthy baby boy whom she named Ariel. We were vastly relieved and exceedingly grateful to hear the doctors declare him perfectly normal in every way. I also felt indebted to the Lubavitcher Rebbe, whose blessing, I felt sure, had served as a protective shield and had been instrumental in assuring my grandson's uneventful delivery and safe birth.

Five years later, I was in my home in Miami when my phone began to ring insistently. Sinaya's voice—garbled, hysterical, frenzied—came on the line, shrieking that she had accidentally slammed down the door of the car trunk on Ariel's head and that he was critically hurt. She screamed for me to rush to the hospital, fast.

As my son drove me to the hospital, I shuddered at the injuries I imagined Ariel had sustained. As our car turned onto the highway, a large white van pulled in front of us and continued ahead of us at a steady clip. Suddenly I began to scream. Emblazoned on the back of the van was an oversized portrait of . . . the Lubavitcher Rebbe! I could not believe my eyes. I grabbed my son's shoulder and pointed to the picture. Seeing the Rebbe's face on the back of that van totally unhinged me. I began to scream at the picture that loomed before me, as if I were addressing an actual person.

"You promised!" I shrieked. "You promised. You said he would grow up healthy and well. Help him! Help me!"

Still, in spite of my suffering, I couldn't help but be struck by the wonder of it all: the strangeness of that van's presence in our lane. All the way to the hospital, the van never changed its course or moved from its position. It remained right in front of us the whole time, never once veering from our path. It almost seemed as if the van were escorting us straight to the hospital door. As soon as we arrived at the emergency room entrance, it vanished from sight.

Inside the reception area, my daughter was waiting in a pool of red, her arms wrapped around Ariel. Pale and frightened, the child was a terrifying specter, hemorrhaging from his head and drenched in blood. When Sinaya saw us, an animal-like howl of pure anguish tore from her lips. Without a word, she thrust Ariel into my arms and ran screaming out the door.

Ariel was bleeding profusely, and soon another pool of blood collected under my own feet. I didn't think he would survive.

But when the doctor saw Ariel, he assured us that his condition looked far worse than it actually was. The blood pouring out of his head was coming from one ruptured vein, and the doctor quickly stitched up the wound. When I told the doctor that a trunk door had been slammed down hard on Ariel's head, he marveled that the child had escaped with such minor injuries, considering the severity of the blow.

"It's a miracle," I said.

One year later, I impulsively decided to attend prayer services at an unfamiliar synagogue in Miami Beach, where I am not a member and where I have no acquaintances. After services, the worshipers were invited to a lavish spread of pastries and wine, and it was there that I first noticed a little elderly man with sidelocks and beard. I have always been attracted to otherworldly types, so I made a beeline to him and boldly introduced myself. He told me his name and that he was a rabbi and a disciple of the Lubavitcher Rebbe. I was excited to share my personal encounter with the Rebbe's miraculous healing powers and told him the story of the blessing, the accident, and the mysterious van.

When I finished my story, his eyes twinkled, and he said, "Would you like to meet the lady who was driving the van that day?" He motioned to his side a woman whom he introduced as Miriam.

Miriam, he told me, had dedicated her life to spreading the teachings of the Lubavitcher Rebbe and, toward that end, had purchased a van in which religious paraphernalia was stored. She had a "billboard" of the Rebbe on the back of her vehicle, so that his luminous visage would bless motorists and pedestrians alike. How far that blessing extended, Miriam could never have known.

~ *Devorah Alouf*

LAST PROMISE

*M*y brother's life had been ravaged by drugs.

We had tried to help him, support him, get him off the drugs. He had served a prison term of three years, and when he was finally discharged, we thought for sure that he'd come to his senses and would start life anew.

Behind bars, James was a model prisoner. He had been rehabilitated and had forsworn the ruinous path he had previously walked. To everyone within earshot, he declared loud and clear that when he reentered "civilian life" he would never go near drugs again. He was so unwavering and fierce in his determination to cast away his previous existence that he became a veritable force within the prison system itself. He discovered that he had a talent for oratory, and he became a motivational speaker. The prison took him to local schools, where he lectured teenagers on the perils of drug addiction. In the penitentiary, James was an absolute star.

But once he got out, something broke inside of him. Within a few short months of his release from prison, the vicious circle had begun again. Many people suspected the truth early on, but I remained clueless. Perhaps it was because he was my little brother whom I loved so much. Or maybe it was because I simply couldn't read what were, for others, telltale signs. But I, for one, did not know that James was back on drugs and in an inevitable spiral of destruction.

One day James came to my apartment with his pregnant wife and two small children in tow. He was utterly broke and asked if I could lend him ten dollars so that he could buy his kids milk and diapers. Because I had no cash on me, I gave him a check for the amount he requested. He thanked me profusely. In fact, his thanks were too profuse. They were excessive, extravagant, and certainly not commensurate with the amount I had lent him. He thanked me endlessly and kept emphasizing over and over again, "Don't worry, Pat—no matter what, I will get you the ten dollars back."

He didn't say it once; he didn't say it twice; he didn't say it three times. He must have reiterated the same sentence at least twenty times.

Finally, I found myself getting irritated by his behavior. This was not characteristic; it wasn't like him to repeat himself in this way. "All right, enough already!" I shouted. "How many times are you going to say the same thing?"

But even in the driveway, as he left with my check, he turned around to repeat three more times: "I promise, you'll get it back."

Only seven days later, James overdosed on drugs, and he was gone—my only sibling. I went to the local florist shop and sadly ordered flowers for his funeral. I couldn't believe that James, my beloved brother, was dead.

I was in such a state of shock, in fact, that I forgot my checkbook at home and didn't have the money to pay for the order. Embarrassed, I assured the store owner that I would return in a few days, when I was more composed, to pay my bill.

The following week, before heading to town, I hunted for the checkbook so that I could fulfill my promise to the florist. As I put the checkbook in my bag, I mused that the very last time I had used it was when I had written the ten-dollar loan for James. Now, only two weeks later, I was again using it to cover his expenses—but this time, it was for flowers for his funeral.

It gave me a chill.

As I advanced toward the door of the florist shop, something fluttered on the sidewalk in front of me.

A brand-new, crisp ten-dollar bill, looking as though it had been freshly minted, fluttered on the concrete. It looked so spanking-clean, so untouched-by-human-hands new, in fact, that I was sure it was either a fake or a joke.

As I bent down to retrieve it, I searched the street for a torn envelope flapping somewhere nearby or an anxious face peering for a lost bill. I could find neither.

But as I picked it up, I knew in my heart that no one would ever come to claim the bill, for the ten dollars was clearly meant for me.

James had kept his last promise.

My brother may have had a lot of personal problems, but he was always true to his word.

~ *Pat Berra Reul Malone*

STANDBY GAME

Chris and Joe* began dating in high school in 1985. It was the first serious relationship for both, and Chris was sure that what she was experiencing was positively, absolutely "true love." The two dated each other exclusively for four years—until they were both in college—and then Chris's world caved in.

One day, in 1989, Joe told Chris that while he cared deeply about her, he wanted to play the field a little . . . test the waters. "You know, we were quite young when we started dating, and the only one I've ever really been involved with has been you," he said. "I think it would be smart for us to see other people. For me, marriage is a lifelong commitment, and we should make sure we're right for one another. We need a basis for comparison."

For the first time in her life, Chris grasped the meaning of that well-worn phrase "a broken heart."

"My heart ached for him last thing at night before I fell asleep and ached for him first thing in the morning when I woke up," she vividly remembers.

Still, she would not deny him his wish. "Deep in my heart I felt certain that he was the one—the only one—for me and that I truly loved him, but I went along with his plan, despite my own misgivings. I never breathed a word of protest or opposition.

* The names in this story, a dramatization, are pseudonyms.

After all, he was the one who had initiated the breakup, and I was too proud to try to reestablish ties."

A year and a half passed. Occasionally, the two would telephone each other just to "check in," but during this entire period, they remained firm about adhering to the provisions of the breakup. Despite the fact that they both lived in a relatively small area in New England, they never encountered one another anywhere, not even once.

In September 1990, Chris was dating a nice guy named Mike, who was known for his spontaneity and joie de vivre.

One evening, he impulsively asked Chris, "Hey, how about driving to Boston and seeing if we can get standby tickets for tonight's Red Sox game?"

Even though they were about an hour away from Boston, Chris didn't mind acting on a whim. "I heard tonight's game is sold out," she said, "but we certainly can try. Maybe we'll get lucky!"

At Boston's Fenway Park, they discovered to their chagrin that the game was indeed sold out, but they decided to wait around anyway. The reward for their exemplary patience was two prized tickets for admission to—yes!—that night's game.

As she settled into her seat, Chris found herself facing the walkway, and it was there that she suddenly glimpsed a flash of familiar red hair. She gulped and thought, Oh, no, it can't be!

But it was.

Her beloved Joe, whom she hadn't seen for eighteen months, was coming down the walkway with his current flame, Diane. All over the small town she lived in, the grapevine had buzzed that the two were a serious "item." Chris couldn't bear seeing the pair together. It was one thing to hear about Joe's active social life and quite another to have to witness it herself. So she looked away and soothed herself silently: Don't say anything, don't greet him, it's okay, he'll probably just walk straight on by and never even notice you . . .

Just then, people in her row began standing up to let a couple squeeze past to get to their seats.

Joe inspected the numbers on his tickets, glanced at the seats, saw Chris sitting next to one of them, and their eyes locked. Joe examined his ticket once again and, jaw dropping in disbelief, reluctantly slid into his seat . . . right next to Chris.

"Well, this is kinda interesting," Chris murmured softly to the shaken man beside her.

But Joe stared straight ahead, unblinking. In an obvious gesture, he opened his program wide, scrutinized it with intense interest, and kept his eyes determinedly on the field without diverting his gaze once. Throughout the entire game, he was uncharacteristically quiet. He didn't talk to his date, Diane, nor did he utter a single word to Chris. He was, in fact, speechless.

Chris could have felt rebuffed and hurt, but instead, she returned home strangely elated.

"Thirty-five-thousand seats at Fenway Park, and he gets to sit right next to me!" she thought. "This has to be a sign."

Meanwhile, Joe's date, Diane, was recapitulating the exact same scene in her mind.

"I knew right then," she told Joe, "we were done."

The next day, an emboldened Chris called Joe and said, "How weird was that?"

They began comparing notes about what they had both been thinking and feeling at the stadium, and they laughed about the coincidence.

Eleven months later, they were married, and their tenth anniversary is coming up soon.

~ *Judith Leventhal*

SISTERLY INTUITION

*L*isa, my six-year-old daughter, was running a high temperature and had a mysterious infection on her leg.

"Have you ever heard of osteomyelitis?" asked our pediatrician gently, when he made the initial diagnosis. This rare bone disease had stricken my precious child. She had to be taken to the hospital, where she would be put on IV medication and observed. If this course of treatment failed, amputation might have to be considered as the next possible option.

It was 1968, and the ward was filled with children suffering from bone cancer. I felt so sad for them. Some were terminal cases. These children would never come home. In contrast, I knew with certainty that I would be bringing Lisa home, either with two legs or one. And for that, I was grateful.

Several days later her infection receded, and we were enormously thankful that Lisa would be coming home with two legs after all and much to talk about with her younger sister Terri.

In her own way, four-year-old Terri had also been a casualty of this medical crisis. Even though I left her under the care of my devoted mother-in-law during the day, Terri still felt abandoned. I would depart for the hospital early every morning and not return until late in the evening to pick her up. The prolonged absence of both her parents and her older sister was a genuine trauma for Terri. When I put her to bed each night after prayers and a story, she would cry for her sister. "Where's Lisa?" she would sob. "Why isn't she here with me?" I promised her that Lisa would be returning home from the hospital shortly and that soon they'd be sharing their bedroom and stories once again.

When the big day came, I was one anxious mom. Despite the fact that she was being discharged from the hospital, Lisa was still forbidden to walk for several more days, and the orthopedic physician warned me to be vigilant about keeping her off her feet. Hard to tell an active six-year-old child, harder yet to enforce!

When Terri and Lisa saw one another, they hugged and kissed, elated to be together again. But during naptime, I decreed, they would have to be apart to ensure that they slept. I sent Terri to the bedroom and put Lisa on the couch in the living room where I could keep her under close watch.

All this time my friend Carole had been keeping me company, and once both girls were safely tucked in, she suggested we take a break over a cup of coffee. I never drink coffee in the afternoon, but my nerves were frayed. Some peace and quiet and a chat with a dear friend, while companionably sipping coffee, seemed inviting. Carole headed to the kitchen to prepare a pot. I welcomed the thought of relaxing a little, for the first time in weeks.

The quiet that had momentarily fallen over the house was suddenly pierced by Terri's wails. She was sobbing in the bedroom. "I want Lisa to sleep here," she cried. "With me. You promised, Mommy. Why does she have to nap on the couch?

You said she'd come back to our room as soon as she gets back from the hospital. I want Lisa!"

She wouldn't let up. Terri continued to weep, whimper, and whine, until I felt I would snap. I had really been tested the last couple of weeks, and now that the crisis was over, my adrenaline had stopped pumping and exhaustion engulfed me instead. A vacation on a small island would be nice, I thought wearily. Having reached my breaking point, I was ready to do anything to get Terri to quit crying and take her nap, so I decided to move Lisa from the couch and let the girls be together in their room.

I had just put Lisa on her bed when I heard a thunderous noise.

My heart raced as I thought: It's the big one. This was it, I thought—the major California earthquake we had been bracing ourselves for all our lives. I ran into the kitchen to get Carole, and we both looked into the living room at the exact same time.

And there, in the middle of my living room, sat a very large four-door car!

Carole and I stood speechless.

A woman and three small children were inside the car, shaken and crying. The woman explained that she had been driving down our street when she had lost control of the car and it had headed straight for the wall of my house. It had penetrated the wall and crashed straight into my living room.

After I helped the woman and her children climb out of the car and made sure that they were not injured, I looked around the living room to assess the damage. It was a complete disaster.

But what really made me tremble was the sight of the couch that Lisa had been lying on only seconds before.

The couch looked like an accordion.

Had Terri not fussed about her sister's absence from their room, I never would have moved Lisa off that couch. And if I hadn't agreed—uncharacteristically—to an afternoon cup of coffee, Carole and I would still have been sitting in the living room when the accident occurred. All three of us—Lisa, Carole, and I—might very well have been killed.

I was still shaking when I called my husband at work. He couldn't believe my story. "Thank goodness, those cars are really sturdy!" he said.

~ *Colleen Ann Traphagen*

BEATING TRAFFIC

*M*y beloved husband, like others of his species (gender isn't strong enough a word to underscore the stark differences that exist between male and female!), takes personal pride in "beating traffic." There is no place for random impulses or spontaneous actions in attempting this Herculean feat. Unlike other well-known male habits (such as frenetic surfing of TV channels on the remote, never lingering long enough on one station to even catch a commercial), beating traffic is an exact science, requiring myriad maps of local roads and now-dusty highways, intense concentration, and savvy understanding of the human race. Beating traffic is a challenge that makes men's hearts race and women's shudder, a warrior's journey that far surpasses that second famous male test of mettle and endurance, otherwise known as "beating the light."

We were winding down after a long holiday weekend in upstate New York, and my husband had spent countless time considering the best way to beat the traffic home to Brooklyn. The final determination was that leaving in the middle of the night (1 a.m.) would achieve that lofty goal. Thus, it was about four in the morning (sigh!) when we finally reached our destination—home sweet home—and thoughts of finally tumbling into bed became less abstract and more real.

Trudging up the steps to our front door behind my triumphant male (yes! he had beaten traffic! no one else was on the road . . .), my thoughts were on the soft pillows on which my head would soon be alighting, the downy quilts under which I would snuggle in cozy comfort.

Alas, it was not meant to be. My husband pulled out his keychain, and then in a dramatic motion more characteristic of me than him, smacked his forehead in rueful recollection and yelped, "Oh, my goodness, I left the house keys on the dining room table!"

Three sets of eyes (my own and those belonging to my two sons) gazed at him mournfully. Then he looked at me and said, "Well, what about yours?" Now, three sets of eyes were fixed on me with trust and hope.

In a small voice, I confessed, "I switched to my white pocketbook (after all, it's Memorial Day, it's fashionably correct now . . .) from my black pocketbook. And I (gulp . . . a little defensively) left the keys in the black pocketbook, sure that you had yours (good, back to offensive position!)."

My in-laws and my mother had copies of our keys in their respective homes, but it was four o'clock in the morning, and we didn't want to wake them. They are over seventy, and it wasn't fair to give them a jolt in the night.

"Okay," my husband said cheerfully, "we've never alarmed the house. I'm sure it's penetrable. I'll go around to the backyard and try to jimmy open the windows."

The good news was that the house is not penetrable. The bad news was that the house was not penetrable when we most desperately wanted it to be.

"Now what do we do?" We slumped on the stairs of our

three-family dwelling. We were exhausted, bedraggled, and too tired to move. We had been up since seven o'clock the previous morning, almost twenty-four hours ago. We couldn't think straight.

"What we need right now is a small miracle!" my husband feebly quipped, semi-skeptic that he is.

Just then, as if on cue, the front door downstairs opened and in trooped our upstairs tenants, a young couple with a baby. They gazed at us in astonishment, and we returned the favor rather impolitely, as our mouths practically gaped open in disbelief.

"What are YOU doing here?" I asked in shock. "Aren't you supposed to be vacationing in New Jersey until tomorrow afternoon?"

"Yeah, well . . . ," the wife shrugged sheepishly. "We were supposed to stay until tomorrow but . . . my husband wanted to beat the traffic!"

Then she became aware of both our luggage and ourselves sprawled across the hallway stairs. "And what about you?" she asked. "What are you doing here so early, and why aren't you inside your apartment?"

"We're locked out . . . ," I moaned. "The keys are on the dining room table. Big problem."

"You don't have a problem at all," she said. "Don't you remember that when I first moved in you gave me your keys? You said that if I ever needed anything, and you weren't home, just to use the keys and help myself?"

I didn't remember. But thankfully, she did.

"Yeah . . . sure I have your keys," she said happily. "And I know exactly where they are. Let me go get them."

As I fell into bed a few minutes later, I said to my husband, "See? You asked for a small miracle and that's precisely what you got!"

"It's a coincidence," he replied.

~ *Yitta Halberstam*

THE REBIRTHDAY

He was as tall as I was short, as black as I was white, as Catholic as I was Jewish, as calm as I was excitable, as Southern as I was Yankee. And for two decades, Bart Rousseve and I had been best friends.

During that time he'd been an usher at my wedding, godfather to my daughter Chloe, adviser through several job changes, confidant to my aspirations, confessor to my sins. I had nurtured him through his painful divorce and his brother's untimely death, cooked him gumbo when he was homesick, helped him decorate his apartment, and even chosen his eyeglass frames.

He was older and wiser. I was younger and warmer. We complemented each other perfectly, but the bond that kept us as close as the pages of a book was a shared faith in God.

We had two rituals. Every January, when Bart would travel to South Africa as part of his job battling apartheid, I would insist that he send me a postcard with a code message on it indicating that he'd come to no harm. And every March, we would go out to dinner alone on a date halfway between our birthdays, which were just two weeks apart.

My husband thought my dependence on Bart was hilarious. "You won't be in touch with him for weeks on end, and then you'll insist on having him over five nights straight just before he leaves for Africa," he'd say.

"You don't understand," I'd reply, "it's not so much that I need to be with him, as that I need to know he's there."

Now, as I sat across from my beloved friend at our annual dinner just before his fifty-third birthday, my worst fear came up and bit me.

"Molly, I have something to tell you," Bart said, reaching across the table and grabbing my hand. "I'm going to enter a monastery. It's too late for me to return to the priesthood, but I've given away my apartment and all my worldly goods, and I'm going to become a Franciscan friar."

Bart had been a Jesuit seminarian. He had reluctantly left just before taking his final vows because he did not believe himself capable of remaining celibate for life. For decades afterward, he'd felt he'd missed his calling, and now that he was older, Bart felt ready to keep his vows. I felt selfish for regretting his news; but how in the world could I do without Bart?

"I know this is the right decision for you," I told him, "and for the greater good of the community. But darn it, what about me? How can you go off to a place where I can't call you every time I have a problem? What will I do without my best friend?"

"You can write me," he said gently. "I'm allowed to correspond with people. Our friendship won't end. It will just be a new dimension in the way we communicate."

"Oh, sure," I said bravely. But that night, I went home and wept. Of course, I tried to see Bart as often as possible over the ensuing months, but he was very busy as a United Nations observer to the first free elections in South Africa. It was summer before we got to spend time alone again. Bart was to leave for the monastery in mid-August. One week earlier, we met for dinner. By coincidence, my husband was out of town on business. After we put Chloe to bed, Bart and I sat on the couch, talking theology. As we were discussing different views on the afterlife, Bart suddenly leaned over and said, "You and I know there is no such thing as death, Molly. It's just a bridge to the next step of the journey."

As Bart left, I hugged him for long minutes, fighting back tears. "I'll miss you," I whispered. "Don't worry," he told me, "I'll still be here."

Those words were etched into every thread of my being as, two weeks later, I got a phone call informing me that Bart had died in an automobile accident on August 14, 1994. "Nobody knows what happened," his sister Katherine told me. "He was driving up to the monastery, it was a sunny day, and there was no other traffic when his car veered off the road and hit a tree. He died instantly. We think he may have had a heart attack."

The priest who gave the eulogy at the funeral said Bart had merely "skipped a step and gone straight to Saint Francis." But that was cold comfort to me. "Bart's dead," I sobbed on my husband's shoulder. "Never," he said firmly. "He is still alive in you."

"I know he's out there somewhere, but I just can't bear to let him go," I confided in Norbu Tsering, a friend from Tibet. He told me that in Buddhism they believe that the soul remains in transition for forty-nine days after death and is reborn on the seventh day of the seventh week. "Since your friend led such an exemplary life, he is sure to have a fine reincarnation,"

Norbu said. "Let yourself mourn him for seven weeks and then celebrate on the forty-ninth day."

I went home and checked the calendar. Bart's supposed "rebirthday" fell on October 2, the same day as my daughter's birthday.

I took solace from that and tried to be brave. But as October approached and we faced the first family birthday in twenty years without Bart, I became increasingly morose. The night before his "rebirthday," I slept fitfully. I awoke the morning of October 2 in a foul mood.

By what I viewed as a sadistic coincidence, my husband and I had to take Chloe downtown to someone else's birthday party that morning. As we tried to get onto the West Side Highway we were blocked by a funeral procession. "Can you believe this?" I raged to my husband. "When's the last time you saw a funeral procession on a highway? This is like some kind of sick cosmic joke."

It was an unseasonably warm and sunny day, and after the party my husband suggested we take a stroll to give me a chance to calm down. We decided to grab a bite at El Teddy's, an offbeat restaurant I had always wanted to try. As we approached, the staff met us at the door and told us the place was closed while they cleaned up from a private party. Then, spotting our little girl, one of the waiters said, "Oh, wait a minute! I have something to give you!" He ran inside and came out with a huge bunch of multicolored helium balloons. In the center was a single silver Mylar globe in the middle that said, "Happy Birthday."

That was it for me. My chest heaved. Tears rolled down my cheeks. "Thank you very much," my husband said quickly and, grabbing the balloons, rushed me over to a nearby park bench. "I've got an idea," he said brightly. "Let's send these balloons up to heaven to wish Bart a happy birthday."

"Oh, yes!" our daughter said, enchanted. "But can I keep one to take home?"

We assented, and after extricating the Mylar balloon from the middle, we released the bunch. "Happy birthday, dear Bart," we sang as the balloons soared into the robin's-egg blue sky and disappeared into cumulus clouds, "Happy birthday to you!"

When we got home, we let the Mylar balloon float to the middle of the living room ceiling, where it remained for a week. Then the helium started to leak out of it. But instead of falling to the floor, as balloons invariably do, this one began floating around the apartment at a height just above my head. Stranger still, it seemed to hover just behind me, wherever I went and at whatever pace.

"This balloon is following me!" I told my husband the first day it happened. He laughed and put the balloon in the kitchen next to the garbage, saying, "Honey, you're nuts."

There was no laughter when we awakened the next morning. The balloon was hovering next to my side of the bed, just above my pillow.

"Omigod," my husband muttered.

"Do you believe me now?" I said.

During the next three days, although I never touched it, that balloon followed me everywhere. When I came in the front door, it would travel from the living room ceiling to the hallway. It traveled with me into the kitchen as I cooked dinner and every time I went to the bathroom. My husband would say, "Hi, Bart," as the balloon floated behind my chair as we sat down at the dinner table. Chloe would call out "Goodnight, Bart," as I tucked her in each night, the balloon bobbing behind me at her bed.

On the fourth day, the balloon became flatter and flatter, moved slower and slower, and floated lower and lower, finally sinking to the floor just inside our front door. My eyes were wet. It was time.

"Thank you, Bart darling," I whispered as I put the deflated balloon outside for the super to pick up. "Thank you for visiting. It was a big help to me. I'm ready now to let you go."

~ *Molly Gordy*

ELEVEN MONTHS

I could barely sleep. Dawn was almost breaking, but I had been up all night, tossing and turning and worrying myself sick over the baby I carried deep in my womb. Finally, as morning came, I confronted my deepest fears. Something is definitely wrong, I acknowledged to myself at last. I must see the doctor immediately.

I had hoped the doctor would pooh-pooh my fears and send me away with the gentle reassurance that everything was all right. Instead, his face reflected the despair I felt, and the news was bad.

"I'm so very sorry, Mrs. Gopin, but you are experiencing an early miscarriage."

I was silent.

In an awkward attempt to console me, he pressed on, "You know, 20 percent of all pregnancies end in miscarriage. These disappointments happen."

It was hard to absorb his words. My five previous pregnancies had all reached full term, so I had no reason to suspect that this one would be any different.

"You're still young . . . you'll have more children." The doctor was trying to be upbeat.

I went home and followed his instructions until the pain and discomfort increased. Later that day I was admitted to the hospital near my home. After several hours of pain and tension, I was examined again and told that the fetus had been discharged from my body.

It was all over.

I remained in the hospital until the next day, which was July 15, to make sure that my body was returning to normal. Just as I was filling out the documents that had to be completed before I could be formally discharged, I began talking to a woman nearby who was also intently filling out forms.

Sally had also had a miscarriage the day before. We didn't know each other, yet the opportunity to empathize with each other's sorrow was cathartic.

"The doctors say that the fetuses that we lose are usually severely deformed," Sally said. "So it really is a blessing that they don't have to be born only to undergo a life of constant physical pain and suffering."

"I know . . . but I still feel so empty inside," I responded sadly.

"I had my own expectations, too," Sally said, and then paused. "But I really do believe that even the pregnancies that we lose have a purpose in the divine plan."

As we were about to part, I suddenly exclaimed, "We'll meet each other again in eleven months. But not here—in the maternity wing!"

Sally smiled. I would have liked more time to talk, but my husband had arrived to take me home.

The following year, on June 13, which was almost exactly eleven months later, I gave birth to a healthy baby girl, delivered by a different doctor in a different hospital in a different city, an hour away from my home.

Just as I was getting out of bed several hours after the birth in order to visit my newborn in the nursery, I passed a familiar-looking woman in the corridor. Goose bumps broke out on my arms. It was Sally, the woman who had miscarried on the same day that I had in the hospital near my home. She too had switched to a new doctor affiliated with a different hospital, and she too had traveled an extra hour to have her baby—a boy, born here . . . two days earlier!

So we had met each other again, after all, but this time we shared our joy instead of our grief, both of us overwhelmed with gratitude that my personal prophecy had been fulfilled.

~ *Sara Gopin*

THE NIGHT SHIFT

*T*t was the last half hour of her shift, and Kim* was tired. She waitressed two nights a week at a local Vietnamese restaurant to supplement her income as a hairdresser, and both jobs required her to be on her feet.

That evening the restaurant in her midwestern city was deserted. The "regulars"—who knew how punctilious the owner was about closing at precisely 10 p.m.—had already vacated the premises, and Kim was busy cleaning up.

So when a stranger walked in at 9:30 and sat down at Kim's table, she sighed.

"Please," she asked another waitress at a different station, "can you take my table? I just want to clean up and get out of here."

The woman was usually accommodating, but that night she too was exhausted. "You take the table, Kim. Come on, you can do it."

Reluctantly, Kim approached the man. She brightened a little when she noticed that he looked as though he came from Vietnam. Even though the restaurant was billed as Vietnamese, many patrons who came to sample the food were just adventurous foodies and had no connection to her native country. But this stranger definitely appeared to be a fellow countryman, and she never wasted an opportunity to press her search.

* The names in this story, a dramatization, are pseudonyms.

Every time Kim encountered a Vietnamese-looking man or woman, she always asked the same question, plain and outright: "Where are you from?"

It had been more than two decades since Kim had started asking strangers this question in the hope of unearthing her long-lost family in Vietnam. And for twenty years, her question had yielded no results.

Now she was tired, exhausted, almost drained of the ability to speak. But the hope that still fluttered in her heart made her press on. "So," she said as she stood at the man's table, order pad in hand, "Where are you from?"

In 1972, during the Vietnam War, Kim had left Vietnam in search of opportunities. Her departure was not a rejection of her family or of her culture but simply a quest for a better life. She thought they would all eventually reunite, and she considered her leave-taking to be temporary. But circumstances rendered her actions permanent. The chaos that ensued in her country in the wake of the war, the turmoil and upheaval that prevailed, had left her as good as orphaned. She had never been able to reestablish contact with the family she left behind, nor locate them through the usual channels.

All these years, she had felt so alone.

In America, on her own, she had achieved many milestones, progressed through different stages: She had married, given birth, gotten divorced. And she had longed for someone close—a mother, a relative—to walk her through these events, counsel her, support her, hold her hand. But no one ever had. Even when she married, in a traditional wedding ceremony, there had been no one to stand at her side. In contrast, her husband had been encircled by crowds of beaming relatives.

The clients at the hairdressing salon where she worked were loyal to her, and her friends at church were kind. But none were family.

"So," she said again as she addressed the stranger, whose name was Vien, "Where are you from?"

"Virginia," he said, and her heart sank. "I'm in town for one day to do some medical research at the university," Vien told her. "I'm staying downtown for the night."

Kim couldn't hide her surprise. "What made you come all the way here?" she asked. "We're so far from downtown."

"Well, I was looking for a Vietnamese restaurant, and I found two listings in the phone book. One was for a restaurant on Park Street, and the other was for this one."

"But the other restaurant is so much closer to downtown," Kim protested.

"You're right," Vien said, shrugging. "I could've just walked there from my hotel, instead of driving here. I dunno. Something just made me come to this one instead. The name sounded good."

"So," she repeated, "where are you from . . . originally?"

"Saigon."

"Me, too," she said. "What part of Saigon?"

He told her the name of the neighborhood.

"Me, too," Kim said, becoming excited. After twenty years, she had finally found someone from her area. "Did you ever know a man by the name of Tran Bac?" she asked, trying to create some frame of reference.

"He's my uncle," the stranger replied.

"No, he's my uncle," Kim said.

Vien and Kim, they discovered, were first cousins.

Kim was frozen in shock. She couldn't believe the coincidence: Vien was in town for one night; he had arbitrarily decided to travel across town to her restaurant; and he had randomly chosen to sit at her table. She worked there only two nights a week, and a half hour later she would have been gone.

Vien was also in a state of disbelief, but for other reasons. His uncle, Tran Bac, was a rich, successful architect, renowned throughout Saigon, and he wondered whether Kim might be some opportunistic, gold-digging phony. So he quizzed her relentlessly about family history and genealogy. When she answered all his questions to his satisfaction, he finally embraced her as one of his own.

Later, when they moved to a Denny's restaurant to continue their talk, Kim discovered that tragedy had struck her immediate family. Her mother had died of heart disease in 1990, and her only brother had been killed in a Cambodian street fight. But much of her kin had emigrated to the United States, and she now knew their whereabouts. In addition to an aunt and a cousin nearby, there were more than two dozen members of her family currently living in several California cities, close enough to visit, with whom she could surely reconnect.

Several months later, Kim traveled to California to meet her long-lost family. Cousins who had been childhood playmates were now grown up and prosperous; once-indomitable uncles were now frail and blind. So much had changed over the years—there was, after all, a twenty-two-year void.

But after initial suspicions were allayed and understandable skepticism vanquished, Kim was warmly welcomed back into the family fold. And even though most of her relatives lived far from the Midwest, Kim now feels that she has finally found the family and the support system she yearned for most of her life.

"This is the best thing that's happened to me," Kim says. "My son is my greatest gift, but you need your blood, too. I needed my family.

"There is a Vietnamese saying that when the leaf flies away from the tree, it is lost. I was the leaf, and I flew back to be with the tree."

~ Judith Leventhal

THE AD

*I*n 1992, I advertised for a husband in the personal-ads section of a local Boston newspaper.

I was pleased with my initiative, gratified that I was not being passive but rather was being proactive about my single status. But all that my action achieved was a series of bad dates and no chemistry. With my optimism dampened after several months of disappointing dead ends, I finally canceled my ad.

I guess I'll meet my future husband some other way, I concluded.

I was sure that my soul mate would eventually show up, but I was thirty-three at the time, my biological clock was ticking, and I was scared and impatient. I was also tired of suffering through awkward dates with men who sounded terrific on the telephone and in their letters, but who were a whole different story when encountered in person. As soon as I met them, I usually wanted to head straight for home—fast!

It turns out that the man of my dreams was married at the time my ads were running, and he was not a subscriber to this local newspaper, anyway. But months later, when his marriage fell apart, he reluctantly reentered the singles scene. He happened to visit an aunt in another town, who gave him her current copy of the local newspaper, suggesting that he check out the personal-ads section. When Stephen glanced at the personals column for that week, he saw an ad that immediately grabbed his attention. He wrote to the mystery lady that night.

That ad was mine. But how was this possible? I had canceled my ad months earlier. By apparent coincidence, the newspaper had erroneously reentered my ad in the one and only personal-ads page Stephen had ever read, long after I had canceled my order.

Stephen and I met the very night I received his letter. He knew instantly that he wanted to marry me. Since his divorce wasn't yet final, it took me a few weeks to come to the same conclusion. Stephen warmed up my cold feet in a short time; his divorce was finalized; and we were married a year after our first date.

I called the local newspaper to tell them of our good news and to ask how my ad had ended up back in the newspaper— without my knowledge or permission—months after I had canceled it. My immediate assumption, when I saw the ad, had been that they were having a slow month and had put in some old ads just to fill out the classified section. My hypothesis, however, was wrong.

Courtney, the employee who handled the personals each week and took my call, knew immediately who I was. She was baffled by my query and responded in genuine surprise. "But I distinctly remember you calling me and telling me to rerun your ad on Labor Day weekend," she insisted.

When I heard her statement, I got a chill. "But it's not true," I protested. "I never called you. How can this be?" We both fell silent as we contemplated the mystery. I was shocked and amazed. "Oh, well," I said lightly, "it must have been my guardian angel!"

To this day, I still don't know who made that call. But it was a true blessing that the "mistake" was made, because I'm married as a result.

~ *Azriela Jaffe*

DEAR ANY SOLDIER

*F*or decades, Abigail Van Buren, the woman behind the venerable and beloved "Dear Abby" advice column, helped the love-lorn, the strife-torn, and the forlorn. Her wisdom and counsel were a source of strength and succor for the millions of fans who followed her column faithfully, a column that is still syndicated today in countless newspapers across the United States, carried on by her daughter. As such, it is probably no exaggeration to state that in many cases, Abby's advice literally changed lives.

In 1995, elementary schoolteacher Rebeka Freeman,* a twenty-four-year-old devoted fan of the advice columnist, was reading "Dear Abby" as she regularly did, when she was struck by a plea inserted in that day's edition. The holidays are approaching, Abby gently reminded her readers, and our servicemen and women overseas are so lonely. It's easy to be swept up by our own whirlwind of business, but let's try to remember them, too. A card or note from their fellow Americans at home would be a special way to let them know they are not forgotten.

Rebeka's heart opened as she thought of how bleak the holidays must be for servicemen overseas. Alone, isolated in a foreign country, separated from loved ones at the most meaningful time of the year . . . she shuddered at the thought of

---

* The names of the couple in this story, a dramatization, are pseudonyms.

their solitariness. She resolved to follow Abby's advice that very afternoon. It's the least I can do, she thought.

"Just wanted you to know there are people thinking about you," she wrote on a greeting card that she addressed to "Any Soldier." She sincerely hoped that her note would uplift the recipient's spirits, whomever he or she might prove to be.

Thousands of miles away at an army base in Korea, Private Dave Fredericks avidly awaited mail call. He relished, indeed yearned for any word from home, and when he was offered a random letter from a sack marked "Operation Abby," he accepted the envelope gratefully. Any mail, even mail from anonymous Americans who had written at Abby's behest, was a welcome reprieve from the loneliness that enwrapped him.

Dave was touched by the warmth Rebeka's note exuded. Impulsively, he decided to write her back. She sounds like such a nice person, he thought. "People like you keep us going," he wrote. He also told her a little bit about himself and the unit he was in.

Rebeka had never expected to receive a response from "Any Soldier," and she was intrigued to learn that the person who had randomly gotten her card was in the 82nd Airborne.

"My dad was in the 82nd Airborne, too," Rebeka wrote back to Dave, feeling that they now shared some common ground, some sense of connection, as a result. But her father had died when she was only four, she told him, and she poured out her feelings of loss in a fresh and honest way.

Dave had also experienced a loss—but a more recent one, one that still hurt. Encouraged by Rebeka's openness in her second letter to him, Dave's own return note also spoke honestly of his painful breakup with his ex-girlfriend. Although geographically far apart, their letters bridged the distance with their warmth and candor.

Things accelerated from there. They exchanged pictures, then e-mails, and finally, long-distance phone calls. The sense that they had both had about each other in the initial round of correspondence was validated, and getting stronger every day.

But would the sizzle of the correspondence translate into great chemistry in person?

It would. It did.

"It was just like a movie," Rebeka sighs of their first meeting four months later. On the second date, Dave proposed, and by the end of that very weekend, they were married.

As an advice columnist, Abigail Van Buren wore many hats—marriage counselor, child psychologist, and social worker were just a few of the functions she performed in everyday life—but this may very well have been the first case where she unwittingly served as . . . matchmaker!

~ Judith Leventhal

THE SIGN

*M*y office was a festive place, where we celebrated each other's good fortune with a joy rarely seen in more competitive environments. Hardly a week went by that we didn't toast someone's award, promotion, engagement, or birthday. Usually I was delighted that my desk was located next to the only counter so that the refreshments and celebrants invariably landed near me.

But not on that particular day. I hadn't confided to anyone at work that I had suffered six miscarriages. But as I watched the pile of baby gifts accumulate for Sally from advertising on her last day before maternity leave, I didn't have to. As the receptionist placed a diaper-shaped cake on the counter next to me, my anguish was so obvious that my boss leaned over and whispered, "Molly, take a slide. I don't want to see you back here until tomorrow."

There are myriad options for women who suffer from infertility, but not for those who can conceive at the drop of a hat yet never make it to the finish line. "Just keep trying," the doctors would say, and my husband and I would regard each other bleakly. Could we bear to risk another cycle of becoming attached to the potential child inside me, only to mourn again in private for yet another loss?

"Help me to align my will with thy will, Oh Lord," I prayed each night. I tried to keep the faith, but eventually I became obsessed with my inability to join the community of parents. Every time I went grocery shopping, to the park, out to eat, or to take the bus or subway, all I could see were babies in strollers pushed by beaming mommies. I slept fitfully, wondering why I couldn't attain what had come so easily to my mother and sister. I knew that self-pity would only deepen my depression. Yet try as I might, I could not escape a growing feeling of resentment, when, shortly before the Jewish New Year in 1988, I miscarried for the seventh time.

In the Jewish religion, services follow a set procedure that parallels the lunar calendar. The Torah—the books of Genesis, Exodus, Leviticus, Numbers, and Deuteronomy—is divided into weekly portions that are read and discussed at exactly the same time each year. This is cause for some consternation among those Jews who only attend synagogue on major holidays, for they hear only the same passages discussed year after year.

Chief among these is the portion read at Rosh Hashanah, the Jewish New Year. For each of the past thirty years, I had sat through New Year's sermons analyzing the chapter in Genesis where God asks Abraham to sacrifice his beloved son Isaac. This year, I let my mind wander. Then the rabbi began reading the portion that always followed, about a barren woman named Hannah. So great was Hannah's grief, the story goes, that the prophet Elijah thought she was drunk when he encountered her on a mountaintop praying that God grant her a child. When he learned the truth, Elijah gave Hannah a special blessing, promising her that one year later, she would give birth to a son whom she should raise to serve God. Hannah agreed, and the baby grew up to be the prophet Samuel.

As the rabbi spoke, this story I had heard so many times before with indifference pierced me like a lightning bolt, and I fled the sanctuary sobbing. Sitting down in a deserted stairwell underneath the exit sign, I poured out all my rage at God. "Tell me," I prayed, "what has Hannah got that I haven't got? Why do you deny me this, when I, too, promise to offer to do my best to educate my child to love and serve you?"

There was no immediate reply. No prophets appeared; no thunder split the sky; I felt no presence comforting me. But in February, my husband and I conceived again, and this time, for some reason, it took. On October 2, 1989, I waddled into Rosh Hashanah services seven months pregnant. But this time I would not be able to hear the end of the sermon either. My water broke, and I was rushed to the hospital to give birth prematurely.

The baby was so tiny that she got tangled in her umbilical cord and choked until her heart and breathing stopped. She was delivered by emergency cesarean section and brought back to life by a gifted team of doctors exactly one year to the day after I had prayed for a child. We named her Eliana—a Hebrew name meaning "God answered me." She remained in the hospital for eight days, and we brought her home on Yom Kippur—the Day of Atonement, which is the holiest day on the Jewish calendar.

"I don't know about you, but I don't need a billboard to get the message here," I told my husband. "One way or another, we are going to send this child to religious day school."

This was an easy vow to make in the passion of the moment, but harder to keep as years went by. When it came time for our beloved child to enter kindergarten, we lacked the funds to pay for private school. We were a whopping $6,000 short of paying the tuition at a school that, at the time, had no scholarship fund. My husband was sanguine. "Look, if it's not meant to be, it's not meant to be," he said. "We'll send her to Sunday school."

I, on the other hand, was troubled. It was Friday, and I went to synagogue for Sabbath services. "Dear God," I prayed, "please send me a sign that shows me what I should do. If you want me to go in another direction, that's fine, but if this is what you want from me, I beg you, please send me a sign."

I left the service feeling strangely comforted. As I arrived home, my husband met me at the door, waving a cordless telephone excitedly. "It's my brother calling!" he said. "He says the lawyer made a mistake in our father's estate, and we're each owed $6,000!"

Not $5,000, or $4,000, but exactly the amount of the missing tuition. "Eli-Ana"—God had answered me again.

~ *Molly Gordy*

FORGIVENESS

I woke up in horror in the middle of the night with sweat pouring off my body. The dream had been so real that I had to pinch myself to realize that I was awake and that it hadn't really happened. I felt an immense weight on my chest, as if I had been sobbing and couldn't get a breath.

I had dreamed that my dad had been in a terrible accident. I could clearly see the waiting room at the hospital. It was strange, because I could see my mother and stepmother sitting together. I remember thinking that it couldn't possibly be happening, because in real life they would *never* sit together. In my dream, Dad—my mentor, my confidant, my port in every storm—died, and I felt this horrible emptiness because I hadn't hugged him for a while.

Dad was a reserved, undemonstrative man who shared his love in quiet, thoughtful ways. He was always telling bad jokes and bragging about how healthy he was. I realized I hadn't given him a hug for a long time—too long. The achy, lonely, and sad feeling persisted until morning, when I was finally able to give him a call. It was such a joy to hear his cheerful "hello."

Immediate relief flooded my tense body. I said, "You have to come visit me today. I'll tell you about it when you get here." He was puzzled, but decided to come on his lunch hour. I waited anxiously until I heard his motorcycle pull up. There was the fifty-three-year-old, trim, business-suited, baldheaded "kid" as he hopped off his new toy.

When Dad came through the door, I hugged him as I've never hugged anyone before. As I held Dad, I felt joy that he was alive and that I was actually touching him. At the same time, I remembered the dream and the experience of sadness and horror that had engulfed me. It was a feeling that I couldn't shake off, and I realized I was trembling. Dad and I looked sadly at each other as I told him about my dream. Dad shared with me that my sisters Colleen and Kathleen had also dreamed about his death.

It was on a beautiful Saturday morning several months later that I got the phone call. Dad had sustained a "few broken ribs" in a motorcycle accident. I called my family and rushed to the hospital, where I was allowed into his room. The shock was almost more than I could bear, and tears welled up in my eyes.

Dad was lying with his eyes closed. He had a large gash on his forehead, and some of his teeth were missing. He had a tube running into his nose and down into his abdomen, and there was blood flowing from the tube into a large bottle on the floor. Although he looked almost unrecognizable, the doctor assured me that he appeared much worse than he actually was. The injuries he had sustained, the doctor told me, were a few broken ribs and slight liver damage.

Dad recognized my voice when I whispered his name, and he told me about the accident and about the woman who had caused it. "Tell her that I forgive her. She didn't mean to hit me," he said, as he arched his back in excruciating pain.

I was furious at this woman who had run over my father. I had no intention of forgiving her.

As we talked, Dad's condition suddenly worsened, and he was rushed into surgery. As his gurney was wheeled past me in the corridor, I grabbed his hand and told him I loved him. As I entered the visitors' lounge to begin the interminable process of waiting, I saw my mother and stepmother sitting together with most of my family. Mom talked about reconciling with Dad before he had gone into surgery.

Four hours later, we were called in to see Dad. He had just gotten out of surgery, had a tube down his throat, a large incision, and had a white, pasty pallor to his skin. I remember screaming, "Is he going to die?" Just then, my sister Diane called from Louisiana. As I spoke to her, he suddenly exhaled as his spirit left him. My dear Dad was gone.

When I had first experienced my dream months before, it was as if I were peering into a window at the future. I felt I had been prepared for Dad's death in order to make our relationship complete. When Dad died, I felt a strange peacefulness, because I had been given a second chance—a chance to hug him, to have deep discussions with him about life, death, and God, and about my own aspirations for the future. Dad had visited all seven of his children before he died and had had similar conversations with each one. The circle was complete.

Afterward, I was tormented by thoughts of Dad's accident. I imagined him moments after he had been hit, lying in the street, alone and in pain. I wondered how long he had had to wait until the ambulance came. My anger at the woman who hit him intensified. Had she been drunk? What right did she have to drive . . . and kill my dad? But Dad's final words haunted me: "Tell her that I forgive her. She didn't mean to hit me."

This was Dad's final request and I couldn't get it out of my mind. I finally found the strength to write a letter to the woman and convey Dad's last message of forgiveness. In the letter, I also faced my grief and asked the questions that had obsessed my mind. How exactly had it happened? What happened that had caused her to injure my dad? Was he conscious after he had been hit and had he said anything of significance?

I was surprised when I received a phone call from her in response. She answered all my questions through anguish and tears. She herself was a nurse and was transporting her very ill child to a doctor. She had halted at the stop sign and then continued driving. She suddenly felt her car strike something and thought it was a dog. When she went to look, she found Dad under the wheel of her car. She had to back her car off of him before she could sit on the ground and place his head in her lap. She told me Dad was comforting *her* by gently squeezing her hand. As we talked, I felt an inner peace. Dad was dead, but his love, forgiveness, and kindness still lived on.

When my sister Diane returned to Louisiana after Dad's funeral, she found an encouraging letter in her mailbox from Dad that he had written and mailed the night before he died. She opened the envelope and out slipped a poem that he had found in a magazine entitled "Life Is Worth Living." She was to cling to that hope because several days later Diane's husband, Frank, was suddenly killed on an oil rig in the Philippines at thirty-two years old. I knew from that letter that Dad was still watching out for us!

Clark A. Acker, I love you Dad!

~ Patricia M. Acker, condensed from
The Dying Teach Us How to Live

FIREFLIES

*T*t is at twilight that I remember Mama best. I can still see her chasing fireflies, her skirt swinging below her knees. As the fading sun slips behind Georgia pine trees, it leaves the sky blanketed with a sunburst of orange. A glow radiates from Mama's face, and laughter dances in her hazel eyes as she gathers fireflies in her hand and shows them to me.

Until I was about five, Mama caught fireflies and put them, still blinking, into an empty mayonnaise jar. Later, she tucked me into bed, and I pretended those pulsating little bugs were a nightlight. Sometimes, they even seemed to be winking at me.

Even at that young age, I was painfully aware Mama never once told me she loved me. It troubled me that she never kissed me good night, or at any other time for that matter. But I knew she cared; she just showed it in a unique way—through humor. I remember her humor being especially poignant as she battled lung cancer. In 1980, Mama began experiencing chest pains. After a few days of pain so severe she had trouble talking, she let me drive her to the doctor.

Once in the examining room, Mama pulled the white paper gown over her head as she was instructed. She held the paper out for my inspection. "I hate these things," she said, a sparkle of mischief growing in her eyes. "I feel like an overgrown paper doll." That was Mama. Though deeply concerned, I laughed out loud.

Later, the X-rays confirmed there was a tumor in her left lung. I had hoped it wasn't malignant, but after a biopsy, the results came back positive. The doctor gave her a year to live.

During that year, Mama battled the cancer by staying busy. With my husband's help, she planted a small garden outside her mobile home on the south side of Atlanta. As soon as the sun blinked upon the horizon each morning, Mama dragged her three-legged stool outside and sat among the green beans, tomatoes, and cucumbers to weed the garden blossoming with life. After a half hour in the blazing sun, perspiration beaded her forehead and upper lip. She'd come in gasping.

Once, with the familiar twinkle in her eyes, she said, "You know, my breath keeps coming in short pants." Then she laughed. I knew what she was imagining—puffs of air dressed in a pair of short pants.

In April of 1981, Mama lay in a hospital bed, her long battle almost at an end. One day after radiation therapy, the nurse wheeled Mama's gurney back into her room. Although a shell of her former self, there was a smile twinkling in those hazel eyes. "My mouth is so dry," she said, "I thought they'd have to shave my tongue." Not only did I laugh out loud but the nurse smiled as well. Thankfully, Mama's humor made accepting her illness a little easier.

One day as I left the hospital room, I couldn't hold back the tears. I felt a comforting touch on my shoulder as I neared the nurse's station. I turned to see a nurse whose eyes showed deep concern. "Why can't you cry with your mother?" she asked. I shook my head trying to regain composure. "It's a shame," she went on, "because every time you leave, your mother cries, too."

I wanted so much to let Mama know I cared, but it was impossible since I'd never received outward affection from her. I simply didn't know how to show her I loved her. As I pondered our lives together, questions formed in my mind. Why can't I tell my mother I love her? Was it because of the betrayal I felt when she left my father? Perhaps it was Mama's growing alcoholism. Maybe she just couldn't handle love and was incapable of giving it. I didn't know. I only knew that I couldn't address my love for her with the words she couldn't say. I couldn't even kiss her.

With the rebirth of spring and the resurrection of the once-dormant azaleas and dogwoods, I found myself thinking of the true meaning of Easter. Although I was alienated from God during this season of sorrow, I remember pleading with Him, please help me say good-bye to my mother before it's too late. Every day I brought my barely used Bible to Mama's room and curled up on a vinyl chair partially hidden behind the hospital bed. One evening when twilight shadows filled the room, I sat in my usual place silently reading from the Psalms.

I don't know who the dark-haired nurse was who interrupted my thoughts, and she had no idea I was sitting there in the shadows. I held my breath as she walked up to Mama. Watching in silence, I saw the nurse gently brush Mama's chestnut hair from her face. She held Mama's face in her hands in the most tender way. I knew she must be an angel sent by God because she did the one thing I couldn't. She leaned down and kissed Mama's forehead. As I gently exhaled, the woman tiptoed from the room.

The next day doctors were forced to increase the dosage of morphine to ease Mama's pain. Through the veil of drugs, Mama's eyes glazed, and I feared I had waited too late to say good-bye. Beneath the green oxygen mask, she struggled for every breath. I struggled with her. She probably won't hear me, I thought, but I have to tell her.

I picked up my mother's spindly hand and held it. I took a sharp breath, and for all the times I couldn't speak, I whispered, "Mama, I love you." For a heartbeat in eternity, Mama's eyes cleared. She looked at me and a smile traced her lips. The presence of God in that room was inexplicable. It was as though God Himself winked at me—like fireflies wink at children on warm, summer nights.

~ Nanette Thorsen-Snipes

LONG-LOST FRIENDS

*T*t was many years ago, but Lorelei Nachin would never forget how scared she felt the day she came to live at the St. Peter's Orphanage in Manchester, New Hampshire. The big building filled with strangers terrified the five-year-old—that is, until she made her first friend.

"Do you want to play?" an older girl, Jen,* asked Lorelei one day.

Lorelei said yes, and from that day on, the girls were inseparable.

But after nine years, the time came for Jen to leave the orphanage, and later Lorelei left, too. Both women were soon married and living in other states; yet a day didn't go by without Jen or Lorelei thinking of her friend. But when they checked with the Manchester City Hall, they were told that the records were sealed.

It seemed they'd never see each other again—until one day, forty-three years later . . .

Lorelei, now fifty-six, was driving near her Florida home when she pulled into a restaurant for lunch. Before long, she found herself chatting with a man who was sitting at a table across from her.

"Where are you from?" he asked.

"I grew up in Manchester," Lisa said. And for some reason,

---

* The name Jen is a pseudonym.

she even gave the address. At that, a woman at the next table stood up. "Isn't that St. Peter's Orphanage?" she asked. "What's your name?"

Lorelei's heart began to race. "Lorelei," she answered.

"Lorelei?" the woman gasped. "It's Jen!"

"Jen!" Lorelei cried. "I can't believe it!"

It turned out that Jen, now sixty-one, had just moved to Florida. "So many times through the years, I wanted to see you again!" Jen cried.

"Me, too!" Lorelei wept, throwing her arms around her old friend.

Today, the women get together as often as they can, and the bond they once felt is back—as strong as ever.

"Having Lorelei back in my life feels like a hole in my heart has been healed," Jen says.

Lorelei agrees: "Now that Jen is here, I think anything is possible. It's like I have my sister back."

- Jamie Kiffel-Alcheh

BERT

*O*ne day my husband had seen "Bert," a homeless man, scavenging in our garbage cans and stopped to speak with him. Learning that he was homeless, he took pity on him and invited him inside for a hot meal. Bert was dressed very neatly and spoke in educated, well-modulated tones. His breadth of knowledge was far-ranging and extensive, and during dinner he regaled us with intelligent and witty comments about politics, medicine, and urban affairs. My husband had deliberately refrained from telling me Bert's background, and by the time dinner was over and the truth was out, my prejudices about "street people" were shattered forever.

Bert was in and out of our lives over the course of the next fifteen years. I learned that he held a master's in physics from City College and had experienced a nervous breakdown in his twenties after his mother, father, and fiancée all died within a three-month period. At first I tried to help Bert. I spoke earnestly to officials at several social service agencies about trying to enroll him in welfare, getting him an apartment or at least a room, and finding him a job. I even made arrangements with a local senior citizens' center to give Bert a free hot lunch every day. But he never kept a single one of the appointments I excitedly but naively made for him—never even put in an appearance at the senior citizens' center, where all that was required of him was that he show up. Eventually I gave up. There was something wizardlike, secretive, and hidden about him, and it seemed as though he possessed a mysterious past that he was trying hard to conceal. In time, I began to accept Bert for what he was. I always opened our home to him and shared our meals with him, giving him cash and clothing whenever I had some to spare. But I no longer tried to change his life.

Bert was pleasant company, jovial and witty, and I always marveled at his optimistic spirit. Despite his bleak circumstances, he seemed to be perpetually in a good mood. It was therefore never any kind of effort or sacrifice to have him around, even though my friends remarked constantly on my so-called altruism.

After fifteen years of hosting Bert without incident, I was startled one day to receive a visit from a neighbor who said she had come to warn me about him. She couldn't help but notice his comings and goings, she said, and she wanted me to know that he was nothing but a common thief.

"How do you know this?" I demanded in disbelief.

"Haven't you ever noticed anything missing from your home?" she asked with a sly look.

"No, never," I replied.

"Well, you're so absentminded to begin with, you probably wouldn't even be aware if something was stolen from under your nose!"

"Why are you saying these things?" I demanded. "On what basis?"

"I saw him in front of a local store the other day. The police were frisking him. He had stolen something from the shop.

And the store owner, whom I personally know, said that all the shopkeepers on the avenue have learned to be wary of him. He has a reputation for pilfering, and he's also said to be violent."

"Are you sure we're talking about the same man?" I insisted, incredulous and shaken.

"It's definitely the same man," the neighbor answered with certitude. "I'd recognize him anywhere. So I came to tell you . . . beware!"

That evening, the doorbell rang, and with a sinking heart, I looked out the window and saw that it was Bert. My husband had taken our two sons to a baseball game, and I was all alone. For the first time since I had met him, I was suddenly afraid of Bert and didn't want him in the house. I stuck my head out the second-story window and yelled, "Hi, Bert! How ya doing?" He squinted up at me, brows knitted in puzzlement. This was not part of our routine; usually, I just opened the door and warmly ushered him inside.

"Uhh, Yitta," he stammered, confused by the obvious shift, "can you open the door? I'm starving!"

I felt anguished. "Oh, Bert, I'm so sorry, I was just about to leave the house this minute for a doctor's appointment."

"Well, do you think you could wait just a little bit while I eat? It's cold tonight, and I sure could use a warm meal."

I thought of the four pieces of chicken and the mashed potatoes on the stove waiting for my family's return. Ordinarily, I would have given Bert my portion without hesitation, but after the neighbor's visit, I found myself gripped by fear. The jovial man who had graced our table for years as a friend suddenly loomed as a stranger whom apparently I had never really known at all.

"So sorry, Bert," I hedged. "Really, I have to leave this minute. But tell you what, I'll pack a shopping bag for you with stuff you can eat."

I raced around the kitchen, pulling out cheese, fruit, and hardboiled eggs from the fridge, crackers, sardines, seltzer, and paper goods from the pantry. When I opened the door and handed the bag to him, his face had a hurt and bewildered expression. I felt ashamed. "Well, thank you for this," he said gesturing toward the bag as he strode down the walkway. "But I sure could have used a hot meal tonight," he threw over his shoulder, before he disappeared.

As I waited for my husband and children to return home from the baseball game, I wrestled with tumultuous thoughts, besieged by self-doubt. *You did the right thing,* comforted one voice. *What are you, crazy? To let a thief into the house! Charity is one thing, and stupidity is another.*

You were wrong to turn him away! strongly rebuked another voice. *He's been in your home for fifteen years, and nothing ever happened. You let yourself be swayed by a vicious gossip. How can you know for sure it was really Bert she was talking about, anyway?*

On and on it went all evening, the verbal sparring between my two inner voices never ceasing, my despair, remorse, and guilt growing with each passing minute. Had I done the right thing? Had I been wrong? How would I ever know the truth?

Finally, my family came home from the baseball game starved, and I began to concentrate on serving dinner. Holding my husband's plate, I began walking toward the dining room table, when I stumbled over a toy on the floor. The plate crashed to the floor, and food flew in all directions. "Don't worry, I have plenty to go around," I lied, planning to give my husband my portion.

The second plate heaped with food had been safely navigated onto the table, when the phone rang. It was for my husband, and he left his place at the table to answer the call. When he returned to the dining room, he stared in astonishment at the sight of our beagle, Flash, perched on her hindquarters, gobbling up his food from the plate. She had been with the family for five years and had never done anything like this before. "Is there enough food to go around now?" he asked, scowling angrily at Flash. "Sure, sure," I lied, wondering how I was going to stretch the remaining pieces of chicken three ways. Just as I approached the stove a third time, the light bulb in the overhead hood inexplicably exploded, scattering shards of glass all over the burners and into the pot of food, which I had left uncovered. Hearing the pop of the exploding bulb, my husband came into the kitchen to investigate, and immediately flung the pot's contents into the garbage can. "Is our dinner jinxed tonight?" he joked good-naturedly.

I began to cry. "Why are you crying?" he chided. "It's not your fault."

"Oh, yes, it is," I sobbed, and I explained what had happened with Bert.

As my husband and boys left the house for the nearest restaurant, I thought of Bert, who didn't have that recourse, who didn't have hot food in his belly to keep him warm through the cold night.

Before the "coincidental" mishaps with the food had occurred that evening, I had wondered long and hard about whether I had done the right or wrong thing about Bert. Had I canvassed my friends for their opinions (which I typically do whenever I'm faced with a moral dilemma), I am sure the answers would have been conflicting, indeterminate, and confusing. Some friends would have reassured me that I was justified in closing both my house and heart to Bert, while others, I know, would have scolded me rigorously for listening to gossip and not giving Bert the benefit of the doubt. My soul-searching would have remained tormented, my quandary unresolved.

But attuned to the message of the mishaps, I knew that I had made a mistake. For in the coincidences, I had found the incontrovertible truth.

~ Yitta Halberstam

THE CUSTOMER

*A*s the owner of the Better Half, a plus-size specialty shop in Brooklyn that has been in existence for thirteen years, I have come to know and love my customers, most of whom are "repeats." Even though they often vow to me that this is the last time they'll be shopping for large sizes because they're enrolling in a gym . . . starting a new diet . . . beginning therapy . . . working with a hypnotist, almost all of them come back regularly. I say this, not with disdain, but tenderly, with affection. I myself am a large-size woman and know the struggle.

Susan Bailey* was a "repeat" customer. An executive with a big real estate company in Manhattan, she would dart into the store twice a year (always in a big hurry), throw suits over her arm (she never tried them on, asserting that she was a perfect size 20 and knew already which cuts of which companies fit her), dash up to the counter to pay, and sprint out to a waiting car. She always went for the best: Jones New York and Harvé Benard were her favorites, and she consistently ran up a tab that totaled well over a thousand dollars. Needless to say, I would get an adrenaline rush whenever she would hurtle through the door (thousand-dollar customers are not easy to come by these days) and would give her my devoted attention. Even though it was hard for me to keep up with her frenetic pace as she sped

*Pseudonym

through the store, I faithfully followed her and serviced her every need, panting for minutes after she had made her hasty exit. Despite the fact that she created a hurricane in her wake, I was always delighted when she arrived. I was gratified that a big-time executive from Manhattan would patronize my humble store, even though I knew it was my huge discounts on designer clothes that were the draw and not my sparkling personality. I was flattered anyway.

One day, I was reflecting about the customers I hadn't seen for a while, when I suddenly realized that Susan Bailey hadn't been around for a long time. A very long time, I thought with a start. Maybe even two years. I wondered what had happened to her. Had she been one of the minority who had gone on a successful diet and maintained her weight loss? Had she moved away? Had someone in the store insulted her unknowingly? Was she shopping somewhere else? I thought of calling her but didn't want to be pushy. Nonetheless, I sent her a postcard announcing a special sale. It came back marked "Addressee Unknown." I felt a twinge of loss when the postcard was returned—where had Susan disappeared to . . . and why?

Every now and then, I leave the store to check out the competition. I make the rounds of all the plus-size stores in Manhattan, trying to spot trends, see which designers are hot, discover new labels. I make these forays two or three times a year. I was on just this kind of expedition one day and was peering into the windows of Jeanne Rafal, a large-size boutique opposite Lord & Taylor on Fifth Avenue, when I heard a plaintive voice behind me. "Please, ma'am, can you spare some change?"

I wheeled around to face my petitioner. My jaw dropped open in astonishment and disbelief. It was Susan Bailey.

Gone were the Jones New York suit, the chic haircut, the flawless makeup. In the place of the woman I had known stood a stranger, disheveled, unwashed, and disoriented. "Susan!" I shrieked. "What's happened to you?"

She didn't seem to recognize me. "Please ma'am," she repeated piteously, "can you spare some change?"

I pulled out all the money in my wallet and gave her forty dollars. As she stood looking at the bounty in her hand with delight, I gazed at her, stricken. "Susan," I said gently, "let's go somewhere to eat and talk." She shook her head no. "Susan," I said again, "don't you remember me . . . the Better Half of Brooklyn?"

For a moment, the cloudy eyes cleared. "Oh, yeah, sure," she said.

"Susan . . . what's happened?" I asked softly in what I hoped was a matter-of-fact manner, trying to conceal my shock and pain at her condition.

"Oh . . ." she muttered vaguely, "the real estate market went bust. . . . I lost my job . . . my mother died . . . my brother stole my inheritance and kicked me out of our house . . . all kinds of terrible things."

"Where are you living now?"

"In a shelter," she mumbled, embarrassed. Then, just as suddenly as it had appeared, the spark of intelligence that had gleamed briefly in her eyes dimmed, and she became muddled and confused again.

"Susan, would you like to come stay in my house for a while?

I have a finished basement where you could live comfortably," I offered.

"No, no, no," she said, starting to back away, looking at me with suspicion. "I have to leave now; I have an appointment. I have to go!"

"Susan!" I pleaded, running after her. "I want to help you. Here's my number—please call me." Apathetically, she took my card.

"Susan," I pressed, "will you call me?"

"Sure, sure," she muttered, retreating quickly.

But she never did.

~ *Yitta Halberstam*

CONNECTIONS

When my son Joey* turned eleven, he was suddenly stricken with panic disorder, which then evolved into agoraphobia. His anxiety attacks were so severe that he spent close to a year confined to his room, while my husband and I searched frantically for a cure. Finally, after eleven months of sheer hell, we found a psychiatrist who prescribed Prozac, a drug that achieved wonders. My husband and I were tremendously grateful that God had returned our son to us from the nightmare world into which he had been plunged.

During this time, we had visited a series of practitioners to determine the cause of our son's problem and had discovered along the way that he was learning-disabled. All the years that he had been in school, no one had picked up on this fact, which we were told may have contributed to or even created the anxiety problem. Now that he was cured of panic disorder, we had to find a school that specialized in learning disabilities. This was not so easy, we soon learned to our dismay. Given his recent medical record, nobody wanted him.

All the schools that specialized in learning disabilities claimed that their students had educational problems, not emotional ones. Our son wouldn't fit in, they maintained; they weren't equipped to handle someone like him. All the psychologists I spoke with insisted that all LD (learning-disabled)

* The names in this story are pseudonyms.

children possess emotional components as a result of their disability, but when I repeated their words to school officials my protests fell on deaf ears. He was rejected by every school we applied to.

There was one particular LD school that I really wanted to get Joey into because it had an excellent reputation and was close to home as well. I had campaigned hard to get him into this school, but they kept turning me down. "Please give my son a chance!" I begged. But nobody wanted to, and I was growing more desperate by the minute.

One evening, I happened to attend a charity event, where I found myself seated next to an older woman named Betty with whom I was vaguely acquainted. I knew her to be a prominent society figure, very wealthy, very influential. Suddenly, before I could think or stop myself, I found myself—to my own shock and horror—pouring out my heart to her about my continuing travails with Joey. Even as I unburdened myself to her, I felt the inappropriateness of what I was doing. "Why are you telling this woman your troubles?" I scolded myself even as I continued to describe my litany of woes. But to my own mystification and chagrin, I found I just couldn't stop. I didn't stop, in fact, until I had completely exhausted every single last detail of my struggle to get Joey into the LD school of my choice.

When I was finally finished, I was appalled at myself. What had I gone and done? But to my surprise, Betty neither distanced herself from me nor looked at me with disdain. Instead, to my complete surprise, her eyes filled with tears, and she patted my hand consolingly, reassuringly.

"Honey," she said warmly, "you've told your story to the right person! It just so happens that I live next door to the founder and director of the school, and it also just so happens that I am one of their major-league contributors. In fact, I have thrown many parlor parties for this particular school and raised tremendous amounts of money. You can consider your son a new student of this school. I give you my word—you can depend on it!"

I couldn't believe my incredible luck, my great fortune! What a godsend, to have been seated next to Betty! Sure enough, true to her word, she used her powers of persuasion and influence, and my son was accepted by the school for the coming year, where he excelled and—for the first time in his life—was placed on the honor roll.

My sense of indebtedness to Betty was infinite, and so I kept up with her, sending gifts and cards. I called her before each holiday to wish her well, and a bond was forged between us. During this time, I learned from other people that she had experienced many problems with her own two children. The older one, a son, was a drug addict who had recently disappeared, and the younger one, a daughter, was mildly mentally disabled and problematic in many different ways. My heart ached for Betty, especially when she inquired frequently about my son's progress and seemed genuinely delighted to learn that he was doing well.

Our relationship continued to develop for about a year, and then Betty's husband died suddenly. I traveled to the suburbs for the funeral, where I would meet her family for the first time. As I stood on the line that slowly filed past the mourning family to offer condolences, I was suddenly struck by a familiar figure sitting beside my friend. "Who's that sitting next to Betty?" I asked the woman behind me. "Why, that's her only daughter, Nancy," she answered, "you know . . . the disabled one." I gasped as I felt goose bumps erupt on my arms. Now everything was suddenly clear. Now I knew for certain why Betty had been fated to be the agent of redemption for my son.

Twenty-five years before, when I had been a high-school student in a private school, a girl with mild mental disabilities had joined our class in senior year. Although our school was not equipped for special ed cases, her wealthy parents had prevailed upon the school administration to give the girl a chance and allow her an education within a mainstream context. Their wealth and influence had overcome all objections, and the girl had been admitted, albeit with great hesitation.

Life in this school, however, was not easy for this young woman. She was viewed as both an outcast and a pariah. She was cruelly shunned by virtually everyone—everyone that is, except me. I had always championed the underdog. I had great sympathy for those on the fringe and had always made an effort to reach out to them—as I reached out to this girl.

On our high school graduation trip to Washington, D.C., no one wanted to room with her in the hotel. I volunteered, and although the experience wasn't an easy one, I was glad that I had done so. After graduation, the class dispersed and separated, striking out in different directions. Some I hadn't ever seen again, some I had forgotten about. Like . . . Nancy.

For it was Nancy who was the young woman sitting next to Betty. It was Nancy, long-lost, long-forgotten Nancy, who was in fact Betty's daughter. During our senior year together, I had never met nor spoken with Nancy's mother, and we had never had occasion to be introduced. Yet our lives had apparently become inextricably connected, our destinies fated to intersect. As the line slowly worked its way toward the mourners, and I drew closer to Betty and Nancy to pay my respects, my eyes filled with tears.

Twenty-five years ago, I had helped Betty's daughter. Twenty-five years later, Betty had repaid the favor and helped me with my son.

Perhaps our own memories are sadly too short, but happily God's is blessedly long.

~ *Anonymous*

THE MESSAGE

*I*n 1991, Debra Robinson* was dating Ed Wilson. They had been seeing each other for over three years. Although he had "popped the question" several times, she had avoided giving him an answer. Fearful, conflicted, and anxious about tying the knot, she kept stalling. As a result, she was tormented and miserable.

One night, Chuck Anton, an old friend of her deceased father, Wayne Robinson, had a dream. In the dream, Wayne said, "Chuck, do me a favor. My daughter Debra is going out with someone, and this person is her destined one. Please find her and tell her that she should marry him and that she's going to have a wonderful life! This match has my blessing, and for once, she should listen to her father!"

Chuck was jolted awake. He hadn't seen Debra Robinson since her father had died ten years before. Shaken, he roused his wife and recounted the dream. She told him it was ridiculous and advised him to go back to sleep. He followed her counsel and soon forgot the entire episode.

A week later, Wayne Robinson reappeared in a new dream. "Chuck!" he expostulated, wagging an accusing finger. "You didn't do what I requested! How many times do I have to ask you to tell my daughter to marry the young man she's seeing!" Once again, Chuck awoke with a start, but this time he resolved to consult his priest.

* The names in this story are pseudonyms.

"Look," said the priest after Chuck poured out his heart. "Find the girl, and ask her if she's currently seeing anyone seriously. If she isn't, say nothing. If she is, you have a responsibility to deliver her father's message."

The following Sunday, Debra Robinson lay on her bed, weeping. The night before, her younger sister Susie had gotten engaged. Although she was happy for her sister, the engagement had undeniably served to accentuate her own sense of aloneness and her anxiety about her relationship with Ed. Debra was in agony and cried out, "Please God, help me figure out what to do! I beg you . . . send me a sign!" At that precise moment, the telephone rang.

"Debra?" an old, familiar voice inquired. "This is Chuck Anton . . ." Three months later, Debra and Ed were married, and they have been living a fairy-tale life ever since!

~ Anonymous

PENNIES FROM HEAVEN

Several years ago, I treated my two grandchildren to dinner at a fast-food restaurant on Avenue J in Brooklyn, in a thriving shopping district. Although it is now closed, at that time a movie theater adjoined the restaurant, and my grandchildren happened to notice the marquee as we passed by. It was displaying the name of a popular Disney movie, one my grandchildren hadn't yet seen. Needless to say, almost as soon as they began tearing into their burgers, they began campaigning to see the movie. Unfortunately, I had spent all my money on dinner and literally didn't have a penny left. I tried to explain this to them, but they were very young and didn't understand. In fact, they began to wail in such a heartrending way that I had to take them out of the restaurant because they were disturbing the other diners.

On the street corner, I went through my pocketbook over and over again, checking every zippered compartment, shaking out every paper, hoping against hope that I would find a ten-dollar bill hidden somewhere, which is all that I required to get us into the movie. But not an extra penny dropped into my waiting palm. As the children's persistent crying rose to a shrill crescendo, I frantically turned every pocket of both the coat and suit I was wearing inside out, but again my efforts were in vain. Nothing. The cacophony of cries issuing from the children was now high-pitched and intense. I bit my lips in distress and muttered to myself in quiet desperation, "Oh, God. If I only had ten dollars. What I wouldn't give for ten dollars right this minute!"

Suddenly, to my shock and astonishment, dollar bills started floating down—seemingly from the sky—fluttering and landing at my feet. Stunned, I looked up at the second-story windows of the store buildings on the street, certain that someone holding the money had looked out a window and inadvertently dropped it. However, no anxious face peered out of any window, and no hastening figure hurried out of any building to retrieve the cash.

Stupefied, I bent down to pick up the dollars, which totaled ten in all—exactly the amount I needed for the tickets—one adult, two children!

I waited for about fifteen minutes to see if anyone would appear to claim the money. When nobody did, and I had satisfied my moral impulse to try to see that the money was rightfully returned, I took the children in tow and headed for the movie. In my head, I thanked my unknown and mysterious benefactor. I paid for the tickets and went into the theater. The movie was just about to begin.

~ *Ettie Grossman*

THE TENANT

wice we had been burned by unsavory tenants living in the basement apartment of our home. The first miscreant robbed us of two thousand dollars, while the second rogue fled in the dark of night owing us back rent for several months. We also had a close brush with a third, who came to see the vacant apartment and expressed an immediate interest in taking it. Thank God for an inquisitive neighbor with a sharp eye and a loose tongue. As soon as he left, she raced across the street. "You know that man who just left your apartment?" she said. "He's wanted in Argentina for murder."

Alas, my husband and I are not wise in the ways of the world, and we are naive when it comes to people. This innocence, which has lasted long past our youth, has provided us with many unexpected blessings and interesting encounters, but it has also furnished us with an overabundant supply of trials, tribulations, and sheer unmitigated grief that we surely could have done without.

"Let's face it," I sighed one day to my husband, as we thought forlornly about the basement apartment, which was—surprise!—vacant again. "The basement is very small and dingy. It only attracts real problematic and troublesome individuals. Let's call it quits as a rental and use it as a playroom for the kids."

"No way," he shook his head adamantly. "We put in a lot of money to fix it up and we need the income it provides."

"It's not worth the trouble!" I argued. "The apartment doesn't appeal to nice, quiet, respectable people. I shudder when I think that we almost harbored a murderer in our very own home!"

"We need the income!" my husband replied stubbornly.

"Can you promise me you'll be extremely careful in checking out the next tenant? Ask for references and so on?"

"I promise. And I'll tell you what. Just to really be on the safe side, I'll try to rent the apartment to a woman rather than a man. Okay?"

"If it doesn't work out this time, I want you to promise me never again," I warned.

"No more heartache," he promised cheerfully.

When an elegantly dressed middle-aged schoolteacher appeared several days later and expressed an interest in renting the apartment, my husband excitedly gave her a lease on the spot and called the local newspaper to cancel the ad he had placed.

"You'll love her!" he assured me, when I expressed my dubiousness about the deal.

"I don't understand this," I said warily. "Why would a well-heeled schoolteacher choose our apartment? It doesn't make any sense. Did you ask her for references?"

"She's so respectable looking, I didn't want to insult her by asking for references."

"What?" I shrieked. "I don't believe this. You promised."

"I know people," he said confidently. "This is a fine woman. You'll see."

One week later, a moving van appeared in front of our house, and movers began heaving furniture into the basement apartment.

I looked for the elegant woman my husband had described, but the person directing the movers with an authoritative air was a young man, neatly dressed in a decent suit. I approached him and asked if he was related to the new tenant.

"That's my mother," he said, flashing a bright, charming smile. "She went abroad for a few weeks, but she said I could use her apartment while she's gone."

The young man looked respectable enough, although I was a little unnerved by his long ponytail and his earring. However, always having given my children long, drawn-out lectures about the importance of looking beyond outward appearances, I was embarrassed not to try to practice what I preached.

"I guess it's OK," I responded. "When is she coming back?"

"Soon," he answered vaguely.

The woman never materialized.

After the first day, the suit never materialized again either. Instead, the new tenant began appearing regularly in torn jeans and tight-fitting T-shirts. A few weeks later, the T-shirt was replaced by an undershirt, and soon after that, he began walking around with a bare chest that exposed several ominous-looking tattoos.

Soon, bizarre-looking characters began drifting in and out of our basement apartment, and raucous music could be heard late at night. My husband tracked down the mysterious woman, who confessed that she had tricked him into renting the apartment to her problematic son, Michael.

"I'm sorry," she said, not sounding sorry at all. "But nobody wanted to rent him an apartment, so I had to do it for him. He's a good boy, don't worry. He won't hurt you."

"Can we get Michael out?" I wailed to my husband day in and day out.

"Even if we have legal recourse, it'll take months. Anyway," my Good Samaritan husband gently chastened me, "instead of focusing on Michael's problems, maybe we should see the situation in a different context. Maybe it's no accident that he landed here, since we've worked with people like him in the past. See it as a test from God," my husband counseled. "Let's invite him for Friday night Sabbath dinner."

Friday night, Michael gleamed like the silver candlesticks on my resplendently set Sabbath table. He wore a suit and was buffed and polished handsomely. He wore a yarmulke out of respect for our Orthodox tradition. (He was Jewish but not religious.)

He helped me serve dinner, engaged in witty, charming banter with my sons, told a few jokes, sang a few Jewish melodies in an enchanting baritone, and even recounted a few Hasidic tales that he remembered from his childhood days.

"Do you see the beauty in this boy's soul?" my husband pressed me after he left. "We can do good work here."

A few weeks later we found out that Michael was a drug addict.

"Now what?" I sighed to my husband.

"Well, the challenge is bigger now, but I still believe we can help him. Now I really know his coming was no accident. God sent him to us, and we've got to help him."

Truly I felt conflicted. On the one hand, I agreed with my husband. On the other hand, I didn't feel that we were equipped to deal with a drug problem. Most important, I worried about my children's safety and the safety of the other children on the block. My husband had confronted Michael about his addiction, and he swore he would hide his problem from the kids. He also gave my husband his word that he would enter a drug rehabilitation program and said that he had already applied to one in California. He also told my husband that as a result of our influence he had started attending synagogue and was thinking about becoming observant. He had sent away for information about schools that specialized in returnees to Judaism, he said.

My husband was satisfied. He didn't entertain for a moment the thought of having Michael evicted, as I had half-hoped he would. Whether Michael was sincere about his intentions or fed my husband the lines he knew would push his buttons, I couldn't be sure. But his promises certainly kept the sheriff's men at bay.

One night I drove to Brooklyn Heights, a neighborhood about thirty minutes from where I live, to take an adult education course. The class ended at eleven, and I asked the instructor for directions back to the highway. I was a trifle nervous about driving home alone late at night, but once I got onto the highway, I breathed a sigh of relief. It would be smooth sailing from here on, I thought.

My relief was premature. To my distress, I suddenly realized that I was on the wrong side of the highway. I was on my way to Queens instead of Brooklyn! I had no recourse but to get off the highway immediately. At the next exit sign, I pulled off the ramp and began searching for an entrance to the Brooklyn-bound side.

I was dazed and disoriented. It would have been a strain even during the daytime, but the misshapen shadows of the night played into my fears. These fears were heightened and compounded by my sudden realization that I was cruising along the streets of one of the toughest neighborhoods in Brooklyn.

"It's OK. Nothing's going to happen," I reassured myself, repeating the words like a mantra. "Just find a gas station, and the attendant will give you directions."

A gas station appeared around a bend. Weak with relief, I pulled into it and honked my horn. Anticipating that the attendant would be out momentarily, I rolled down my window to talk with him. Instead, five menacing figures stepped out of the station's shadows and encircled my car. The attendant was nowhere to be seen.

"Need help, lady?" one man growled, as I cautioned myself to look beyond appearances.

"Hi, good evening, how ya doing?" I said brightly, deciding that the cool "I-am-not-scared of you, you are God's divine creature just as much as I am" approach might work here.

"Could you please tell me how to get onto the BQE going west?"

"Sure, honey, I'll be glad to," the man said, and for a fraction of a second my fears were allayed. "But it'll cost you . . ." he added with a growl.

The menacing figures moved closer to the car.

Suddenly, a new figure detached itself from another throng of men huddled in a corner of the gas station and raced toward my car.

"I recognize that voice. . . . It's Mrs. Mandelbaum! Mrs. Mandelbaum, Mrs. Mandelbaum, how ya doin'?" the voice inquired serendipitously.

It was Michael.

He approached the men encircling the car and scowled at them threateningly.

"What're you bothering this nice lady for? She's my landlady. Leave her alone! Scram!"

Reluctantly, the men walked away from the car, giving it and me one last lingering look.

"Mrs. Mandelbaum, what are you doing here?" my savior inquired blithely.

"Michael, what are you doing here?" I countered.

"Oh, I come here to do some business," he answered vaguely.

"Want a lift home?" I asked.

"Nah, thanks, but I'm not finished here yet."

"Michael, you probably saved my life. I don't know how to thank you."

"Well, you've been valiantly trying to save mine, so I guess we're even now," he said in a light tone.

A few weeks after the gas station incident, Michael left for a rehabilitation center in California. I haven't seen him since, but I pray that God will continue to protect the man who protected me the night I took a wrong turn off the highway.

— Yitta Halberstam

THE DRESS IN THE WINDOW

*I*f there was one thing on which their friends agreed, it was this: Brenda and Adam would never get married. They were both practical people, not romantic. Ask them about marriage, and they shrugged: Why bother? It's a meaningless ritual.

One night, Brenda and Adam decided to take a stroll. The mood between them was unsettled. Recently, after seven years together, they had split up. The separation was painful, and now they were cautiously experimenting with dating each other again.

They began their stroll downtown in Greenwich Village. It was a hot July night, and the streets of New York City were alive with young couples. Brenda and Adam walked aimlessly, gazing at the shop windows.

They wandered for hours. The pleasure of each other's company was so great, they didn't notice the miles vanishing under their feet. They drifted north through the chaos of Times Square, the crush of opera patrons at Lincoln Center, the crowds of moviegoers thronging on upper Broadway.

At midnight, they meandered onto a deserted boulevard. After so much hubbub, the darkness was eerie. Across the street, one solitary light beckoned.

"Come on, Adam," said Brenda. She pulled him toward the golden light emanating softly from a tiny shop. Illuminated in the store window was a dress so magnificent they both stared at it, transfixed. It was a simple white dress, gossamer as fairy wings.

"Did you ever see such a beautiful dress?" gasped Brenda.

"You know, Brenda," said Adam, "if you ever wore a dress like that, I'd have to marry you."

A bolt of electricity ran through Brenda. Could this be Adam? The man who always told her that in today's world marriage doesn't hold water?

"You better watch what you say, Adam," she answered. "I might think you mean it."

At that moment, the shop door swung open. A scrawny old woman, a cigarette dangling from her mouth, impatiently waved them inside. "I understand you're getting married," she said. "Come in."

As if in a dream, they followed her.

"Try it on," said the old woman. Brenda stepped into the dress. It fit as perfectly as the slipper had fit Cinderella.

Brenda took off the dress. Still in a trance, they thanked the woman and left.

"So I guess that's it," said Adam. "When should we set the date?"

Somehow the dress had settled everything. They were getting married, and that was that. But as they walked along, planning their wedding, Brenda felt her usual practical personality resurfacing.

"Listen, Adam, that dress cost twelve hundred dollars! It doesn't make sense to be so extravagant for something we'll use only once."

"Don't worry," said Adam. "Our daughter will wear it when she gets married."

Again, Brenda stared at him in shock. This was Adam? Her frugal, unromantic Adam?

The next morning, Brenda raced to the dress shop. "I want that dress," she told the two young shop girls.

"Okay," they said. "But try it on first."

"I don't need to," said Brenda. "I was here late last night. The older woman let me in."

"What woman?" The two girls stared at her, amazed. "There's never anybody here at night."

"Well, last night there was," said Brenda. "Around midnight."

"That's impossible," said the girls. "There's no way anyone was here."

"Look," said Brenda, "I'm absolutely positive that . . ." At that moment, the phone rang. The designer of the dress was calling, the very woman who had let in Brenda and Adam last night.

The conversation that followed was remarkable. It turned out that the old woman, who owned the shop, had not been there in years. She hated the store, and in fact, she was planning on closing it. But the night before, in her downtown shop, she had finished sewing the white dress. And she was so thrilled with her creation that she had felt compelled to rush to her uptown store and display it. Just a few minutes after she had placed it in the window, Brenda and Adam had strolled by.

Brenda was stunned. Was it more than mere chance that had led them to that fateful dress? It almost seemed as if something had been pulling them toward it, something that had pulled the old woman, too. Or was it all just coincidence?

Two months later, Brenda glided up the steps of City Hall, lovely as a princess in her white dress. Striding by her side was a tuxedo-clad Adam. Without a doubt, they were the best-dressed couple getting married in City Hall that day. And as they exchanged their vows, Brenda couldn't help wondering: Without this dress, would we ever have married? Or would we have stayed our practical, unromantic selves forever?

One year later, the topic of the dress came up again. Their friends had gathered to admire their newborn baby, a girl whom Brenda and Adam hoped would someday wear the wedding dress, too.

"You know," said a friend, in between cooing and making faces at their adorable baby, "I still can't get over the fact that you two got married. You just don't seem the type."

"We're not," said Brenda. "It's just that we saw this dress . . ."

- Peggy Sarlin

THE PRAYER

*E*verybody in the family noticed the special bond between Nana Rizzo and her two-year old granddaughter, Andrea. The two of them could sit happily on the floor together for hours, laughing and playing, lost in their private world of make-believe. And when playtime was over and Andrea climbed on Nana's lap to kiss her goodnight, everyone marveled at how much they looked alike.

On Father's Day, Nana Rizzo came for a family barbeque. The day passed pleasantly. The grown-ups chatted, while Andrea and her cousins ran around the backyard. When night fell, the older children went inside. The grown-ups lingered on their lawn chairs enjoying their conversation as Andrea played nearby, drawing with chalk.

Nobody noticed Andrea on her hands and knees, leaning over the pool to dip in her chalk. Nobody heard Andrea fall in. Nobody saw Andrea lose consciousness as she drowned.

Suddenly, Nana let out a scream. "Andrea's in the pool!"

In a flash, Andrea's mother, Barbara, was in the water, pulling her out. Andrea was not breathing. Her skin was blue. Her little body was limp and still.

Pandemonium broke out. Everyone began shrieking, crying, running around frantically. Barbara leaned over her daughter and desperately breathed into her mouth, performing CPR. But it was no use. Andrea was lifeless. Nothing they did could bring her back.

Nana Rizzo closed her eyes and whispered a prayer.

"Dear God, I'm an old woman. Take me, not her."

In the next backyard, Sam Callahan listened to the shrieks coming from the other side of the fence, puzzled. Was that the sound of a wild party or something wrong? He didn't live here; he didn't know these people. He was just stopping in for a quick Father's Day visit to see his dad.

"Well, I might as well check it out," he thought.

As soon as he saw the terrified family bending over a lifeless child, he sprang into action.

"Did you do the Heimlich maneuver?" he asked Barbara.

When she answered no, he grabbed Andrea from behind and gently squeezed below her ribs. A stream of water gushed from her mouth. Quickly, Sam gave her two breaths.

Andrea's eyes fluttered open. The color flooded back to her cheeks, and she began to cry.

"Mommy! I fell in the pool!"

Everyone started sobbing again, this time for joy. Nana Rizzo kissed the top of Andrea's head then looked up at the sky.

"Thank you, God," she whispered. "Thank you for answering my prayer."

Still holding Andrea tight, Barbara turned to the stranger who had saved her child.

"You're my guardian angel! How can I ever repay you?"

Sam shook his head. "You don't have to repay me."

"But how did you know what to do?" asked Barbara.

"Oh, I was a lifeguard for many years. I'm just thrilled I happened to be here."

In the days that followed, life quickly returned to normal. Andrea suffered no damage from her terrible ordeal and was soon as playful as ever. Barbara, while deeply shaken, found herself drawn back into the usual rushed routine of work and errands and constant never-ending motion.

Only one person did not return to normal . . . Nana Rizzo.

For her whole life, she had enjoyed robust good health. Now, mysteriously, she began to fade away. Her energy deserted her; pain kept her up at night.

When Barbara took Nana to the doctor, he privately confirmed her worst fears. Nana had cancer. The end would be swift and soon. And it would be unbearably painful.

As Nana's health rapidly deteriorated, the family grew frantic. No one could stand the thought of the suffering she would endure. Yet Nana remained strangely calm, even serene.

"Don't worry," she said. "God has answered my prayers."

On August 25, two months from the day that she asked God to take her life and spare Andrea's, Nana Rizzo died peacefully.

A short while later, Andrea woke up crying. Barbara ran to her room and scooped her into her arms.

"What's wrong, Andrea?"

"Mommy, I keep dreaming I'm in the pool."

"And I get you out, right, Andrea?" said Barbara.

"No, Mommy. In my dreams, it's Nana Rizzo who lifts me up."

~ Peggy Sarlin

STRANGERS ON A BUS

"Wherever you go, there you are," says the song. But for Carrie Moore,* the lyrics should have been changed to "Wherever you go, there's Matt Lyons."

New York City is often seen as a huge, impersonal metropolis where hordes of strangers robotically stream past each other, never to meet again. Not to Carrie. To her, New York was a small town in which she kept bumping into Matt Lyons over and over again.

The first time she noticed him was waiting for the crosstown bus. He was hard not to notice, being handsome and six feet two inches tall. But what drew her attention was not his good looks. "There's someone who looks happy," she thought, not knowing that he was stealing sidelong glances at her and thinking, "What an exuberant-looking girl!"

Throughout the fall of 1996, Carrie and Matt kept spotting each other around the neighborhood: drinking with friends at a bar, waiting for bagels, eating dinner at the local grill. Gradually, their relationship progressed. When they saw each other on the bus or sidewalk, they no longer pretended they didn't notice. Instead, they nodded quickly, almost imperceptibly, at each other, as if to say, "Hey there. I sort of know you." Carrie's friends began teasing her about her "bus boy," while Matt's friends ribbed him about "the cute girl in my neighborhood."

* The names in this story, a dramatization, are pseudonyms.

One June morning in 1997, Carrie stepped into her office elevator. It was rush hour, a time when the elevator was always packed. But on this morning, only one person entered: Matt Lyons. As she looked at him in astonishment, the doors closed, and for the first time, they were alone.

"I don't think we've formally met," said Matt. "I'm Matt."

"I'm Carrie," she said.

That was all there was to the incident, but looking back upon it, Carrie now thinks it was God's way of telling them that they should get to know each other.

Two months went by before they met again, this time on the crosstown bus. Matt was with a friend, and the three of them chatted pleasantly. "Who is that?" Matt's friend asked him, as soon as Carrie left. "Why don't you ask her out?"

"But I don't really know her," said Matt. "She's just someone I see around."

That did it. Carrie had mentioned where she worked during their conversation on the bus. Matt called her office, asked to speak to a woman named Carrie, and invited her to lunch.

Right from their first date, they discovered how much they had in common. They lived three blocks apart. For the last five years, they had worked in the same building. They both loved golf, went to Mass every Sunday, and were fanatically neat.

"I do have a pretty strange hobby though," Matt confessed. "I play the bagpipes."

Carrie let out a shriek. Her whole family was dedicated to Irish step dancing, and to her, bagpipe music was better than rock and roll.

As their romance blossomed, the time came for Carrie's family to meet Matt. In yet another connection between them, the location for the family gathering was eerily convenient: Matt's apartment was directly across the street from her aunt and uncle, on exactly the same level. At the party, Carrie's ninety-eight-year-old grandmother expressed a yearning for bagpipe music. Matt ducked across the street. An hour later, he returned, dressed in full bagpipe regalia, ready to tirelessly oblige Grandma's every request. Her family happily conceded: Here indeed was Carrie's dream man.

At their wedding, Matt played the bagpipes while Carrie step-danced jubilantly with her sisters. "I can't believe it," she said. "I'm married to the stranger I met on the bus!"

~ Peggy Sarlin

LOST AND FOUND

*B*rooklyn College issues photo ID cards to all its students, which they must show to security guards at the entrances to various buildings on campus. Thus, I was utterly dismayed one evening when, at the entrance to the library, I reached into my wallet for my ID card and discovered to my shock that it wasn't there! Although I begged the guard at the door to let me in because I had a paper due that required extensive research, my pleas fell on deaf ears. Fuming, I berated myself for having lost the ID card and wondered how and where it had gone astray. I seemed to recall having taken my wallet out of my pocketbook sometime during the day, probably en route to work in Manhattan, but after that I drew a blank. I was annoyed at myself, because the process of applying for a new card was a bureaucratic nightmare, with hours of waiting on line for the application, for the photograph to be taken, for the ID card to be validated, and so on. Worst of all, the offices where I would need to go for help were only open during the daytime. I was an evening student and worked full-time. I would have to take a day off from work, and I had just started a new job.

I returned home later that night, still in a bad mood, still chastising myself, still wondering how I would approach my supervisor about a day off. As I walked through the door, the phone rang. It was my best friend, Toby.

"Guess what I found today at a subway station in Manhattan?" she crowed. "You're going to get a kick out of this!"

"Oh yeah, what?" I asked, uninterested, grumpy, and still obsessing.

"Your ID card!"

"What!" I screamed. "That's incredible! Where'd you find it?"

"At the Thirty-Fourth Street station of the B train. I saw a piece of paper lying on the floor, and something just made me bend down and pick it up. Imagine my astonishment when I saw that—of all things—it's my best friend's picture!"

We both agreed that her retrieval of my ID card had been a minor miracle, and chalked it up to one of life's undeniable mysteries.

Just as she was about to hang up, I suddenly had a thought. "Toby . . . wait a second . . . it just dawned on me . . . You don't usually take the B train to Manhattan, do you?"

"No," she said, "but there was some mechanical trouble on the N train that I was originally on, and it was taken out of service. I waited around for another one, but when twenty minutes had passed and there was still no train in sight, I got frustrated and lost patience. So I walked through the station to switch to the B."

"Toby, do you realize," I said excitedly, "that if you had waited for the N train you would never have found my card?"

~ *Yitta Halberstam*

MY EDITOR, MY FRIEND

*T*was attending social work school when I got the assignment that changed my life. The professor instructed that we write a fifteen-page paper on a client's case. He asked us to write about the case in minute detail. I felt stressed just thinking about it. Then he dropped the bomb. "Make copies of your paper to be given to each student in the class." My blood went cold.

I had written plenty of papers for school, but they were meant only for the teachers' eyes, never my peers. I had always harbored insecurities about my writing. And each paper I handed in carried with it a barely tolerable degree of trepidation. But, this one really upped the ante. Now my writing would be laid open for all to see.

Every time I sat down to start the paper, my insecurities reigned supreme, and my fingers promptly froze. I hadn't a clue about how to overcome this deadlock. An idea flashed in my head. "I'll get an editor!" Then my doubts kicked in. "But, where will I ever find an editor? And how can I possibly afford one?" Bereft of answers, I quickly ushered the fantasy out and made another attempt at getting back to work. Again, it failed. I welcomed the idea of somehow meeting an editor back to my thoughts and to my surprise, it actually comforted me.

While conducting research for the paper at Manhattan's mammoth Fifth Avenue Library, I found myself stumped by a particular question concerning the case. I telephoned a classmate for assistance. I enumerated the points I had thus far come up with and explained how I planned to formulate those ideas. I realized that the classmate felt incapable of helping me out of my dilemma. I thanked her and hung up. Just then, an older, diminutive woman waiting near the phone looked up at me and said with a determined air of authority, "You are coming from the wrong angle."

"What?" I asked, perplexed and a little annoyed. "Were you just listening to my conversation?"

"It doesn't matter," she said. "You are definitely coming from the wrong angle."

I wasn't sure whether to be amused or intrigued. "Well where do you think I should be coming from?"

She went on to give me one of the greatest lessons on writing I had ever experienced. I could see she evidently knew how I should approach this paper.

"Where did you learn to write so well?" I asked.

"It's my job; I'm an editor."

She told me her name was Henrietta Yusem and she worked for what was then called Harcourt, a major publishing house. I couldn't believe my good fortune. A few hours prior, I had prayed for an editor and here I stood face-to-face with this kind and competent woman, who was more than willing to provide me with what I needed—her masterful writing expertise. Still positioned in front of the library pay phone, Henrietta provided me with the perfect angle for my paper.

"Now go write!" she half scolded me, as though she knew me all my life.

"Can we meet again so that you can review it and edit it?" I asked, hoping against hope.

"Of course," she smiled.

We decided where and when to meet, and that was how my magical friendship with Henrietta began.

At the time, I lived on the Upper West Side. Henrietta lived just a few blocks away. She kept her promise and came to edit my paper. She told me that her price would be my commitment to do the best job I was capable of doing. On the day of our second meeting, I handed her my fifteen-page paper with a significant amount of anxiety. I sat down opposite her so that I could catch her facial expressions as she read my paper. She finally finished the piece, and I held my breath, suddenly wishing I had never given it to her.

"If I were grading you, I would give you an A+."

"What?" I exclaimed. "Do you really mean it?"

"Of course I mean it," she insisted. "This is excellent." A surge of confidence flowed like an electric current throughout my body. I thought that if Henrietta could believe in me, then I could too.

From that life-changing moment, my battle with school papers ended. I gleaned confidence from a magical encounter with a good-hearted stranger, who was a stranger no more. We became fast friends. In fact, Henrietta insisted that we stay in touch by writing letters. Hers came brimming with wisdom. I welcomed her constant guidance and support. Sometimes she sent along photographs and poetry, always with a loving touch.

In an age inundated with technology, with answering

machines, faxes, e-mail, and the like, I had found a comforting reprieve amid the turmoil. I looked forward to those handwritten letters from my dear friend just blocks away. I saved each letter as I would a jewel, knowing that one day, these limited treasures would cease.

Henrietta spent the last year of her life in a nursing home. Preferring not to be seen in her feeble condition, she asked me not to visit. She wanted us to continue to write one another. In keeping with our tradition, Henrietta's brother, Sy, also wrote me letters. In one such letter he informed me that whenever he would visit his sister, he would read to her from my first published book, *Small Miracles*, and that it brought her immeasurable moments of happiness.

Henrietta was my first editor, sent to me from above. She gave me a priceless gift—the confidence to express myself in writing. Henrietta taught me that we can slow down life's dizzying velocity to a more human-friendly pace, and that, in a city where faces stream by in endless anonymity, we can manage to make a meaningful connection if we only try.

Henrietta passed away on November 12, 1998. I miss her. Henrietta, this one's for you.

~ *Judith Leventhal*

THE ELECTRICIANS

*T*imes were bad in Israel; the economy was struggling. It was difficult for anyone—the credentialed and unskilled alike—to get a job. All over the country, people were out of work, and housewives turned frugal and penny-pinching.

In this climate, Henya Lerman* knew that she was indeed lucky to have found employment at a stable and well-respected company in a suburb of Tel Aviv. Henya considered herself not only fortunate but also blessed: The man who owned the company was an Orthodox Jew named Heshy Fleisher, who was very sensitive to his employees' needs. Still, Henya couldn't help but worry. She was pregnant, due in three months, and wondered: Will the boss grant me maternity leave and keep my job open until I'm ready to return to work?

Various scenarios played out in her head, and she fretted about the possibilities that loomed before her. Her husband had been out of work for over six months, and her brother, who lived with them, was also unemployed. Right now she was the sole breadwinner of the family of three—soon to be four. The emotional burden was enormous.

Even at the annual company dinner—a lavish event that Mr. Fleisher arranged each year to honor and thank his employees—Henya couldn't stop agonizing. During a lull in the conversation, she began confiding her concerns to her

* The names in this story, a dramatization, are pseudonyms.

colleagues. They cast warning glances in the boss's direction, but Mr. Fleisher's presence at the table didn't seem to dampen her volubility. Her coworkers began to shift uncomfortably in their seats, embarrassed by Henya's indiscretion. Perhaps she was desperately seeking their reassurance—or Mr. Fleisher's—but she certainly seemed to have blundered into a major faux pas.

Mr. Fleisher, however, was not as discomfited as his staff. He regarded Henya not with annoyance but with compassion and carefully switched the topic.

"Now that we're all here together," he said in a warm and friendly voice, "we have the rare opportunity to really get to know each other better. We are, thank God, so busy at work we never have time to talk. I feel bad that I know so little about my own staff. Where is everyone from originally, anyway?"

The segue was anything but smooth, but everyone at the table was relieved to change the topic. People began talking eagerly about their respective pasts, backgrounds, histories. Hardly anyone at the table was a Sabra (native-born Israeli).

"And where are you from, Henya?" Mr. Fleisher asked encouragingly.

She told him the name of her old neighborhood in Brooklyn. "It was once a thriving section of the city but it deteriorated into a bad area," she answered shyly, still mortified by her blunder. "None of my childhood friends live there anymore."

While Mr. Fleisher had been responsive to all of his employees' stories, it was Henya's reply that seemed to strike a chord. He began to bombard her with a series of rapid-fire questions.

"Where exactly did you live? When did you live there? What were your parents' names? Are they still alive? What shul (synagogue) did they attend?"

Mr. Fleisher could barely contain his excitement; Henya could barely conceal her surprise. The staff members kept looking back and forth at the two of them in bewilderment. Their confusion was compounded by the fact that Mr. Fleisher's eyes had begun to well up with tears as he suddenly stood up and excused himself from the room. When he returned his eyes were red-rimmed, and he appeared overcome by emotion.

He turned to Henya and said, "I want to tell you a story. Many years ago, two electricians lived in an old Jewish neighborhood in Brooklyn. One of them was a member of the electrician's union and was very successful; the other had been unable to join the union and had been having a difficult time earning a decent wage. He was reduced to doing odd jobs that brought in very little money.

"Despite the differences in their lifestyles, the two became close friends. They davened (prayed) in the same shul and often walked home together. They promised they would introduce their families to one another, but somehow they never did.

"One day the poor electrician was suddenly stricken with a heart attack, and after a few days of touch-and-go, he died. When the wealthy electrician came to pay the family a shiva (condolence) call, he observed with sadness the destitute surroundings in which his friend had lived: the meager furniture, the scanty possessions, the frayed couch. He gently asked the widow if she had enough food at home for herself and her children, and she quickly said yes. But when he went to the kitchen, he inspected the cupboards and refrigerator and saw that both were bare. So every single night during the seven-day period of shiva, when the house was full of visitors and the widow was distracted, the electrician would sneak into the kitchen and stock the empty shelves with food.

"Two months later, the widow called the electrician and told him that her basement was full of all kinds of electrical supplies that her husband had used and that she would like to sell him its entire contents for $100. The electrician promised he would come over that night and take a look, and he was dumbfounded at the sheer quantity of what his friend had amassed over the years. Much of it he deemed worthless, but scattered among the paraphernalia that littered the basement floor seemed to be a few items of value. The electrician told the widow that he would need some time to sort through the collection and assess its worth.

"For three weeks the electrician came nightly and labored for hours in the basement, sorting through the piles and heaps and layers of equipment, tools, and machinery; he separated the junk from the surprising treasures and organized them into categories that would only make sense to other members of his trade. Unbeknownst to the widow, he had absolutely no intention of paying her the $100 that she had requested and then taking off with the stuff. In his mind, he had engineered an entirely different plan of his own.

"When he had finished his massive undertaking, the electrician called all the contractors, builders, and jobbers he knew and told them that he was conducting a sale on the following Sunday of various electrical supplies that they could use in their work. The sale was enormously successful, bringing in more than $3,000—a princely sum in those days. Needless to say, the electrician did not take the money for himself, but instead he handed it over to the widow and her children. This revenue helped sustain the family and keep them afloat for many months."

Mr. Fleisher ended the story with a heartfelt sigh and turned to Henya Lerman.

"Now let me introduce the cast of characters in this story. The incredibly kind electrician . . . that was your grandfather. The young orphans . . . one of them was me. For it was my father who passed away, and it was your grandfather who saved us. Your grandfather's righteousness and charity saved my family's life."

Mr. Fleisher continued emotionally, "Mrs. Lerman, you never need worry about *parnosa* (income) again. I promise that you will always have a job in my company. And if your husband and brother will please be so kind as to come to my office tomorrow, I will find them both jobs, too."

Later that night, Henya wrote a letter to her grandfather, still alive in America, in which she recounted the episode, ending, "Thank you, Grandfather. I am so proud to be your grandchild. You not only saved this man's family, you saved mine."

~ *Yitta Halberstam*

PRAYERS

I thought my marriage was idyllic. I thought my husband was a respectable, upright, law-abiding citizen. I thought we had an open, honest relationship in which we knew everything there was to know about each other.

But when I discovered the cache of drugs hidden in his briefcase one day, I realized that everything I had assumed about my husband and about our marriage had been a total sham.

Fifteen years of pretense came crashing down around me as I examined the small plastic bags of cocaine stashed in the pouch compartment of his case. How had the truth eluded me all this time? How could I have been so naive? How could I have lived with a hard-core addict and not even known?

It was not the shock of discovering that he was an addict that pulled me away from him irrevocably. I could have lived with the knowledge that my husband had a serious problem; I am a loyal person, and I would have given him my support. Together, we could have attempted to surmount the crisis. But the realization that he had lied to me for who-knew how many years, perpetrated constant deceptions, engaged in endless subterfuge in order to sustain his habit and hide it from me— that realization I simply could not countenance.

For me, honesty between partners was the paramount thing; without it there could be no relationship.

So there I was, a newly divorced forty-year-old with five children on my hands, and no marketable skills. All my life, I had devoted myself to home and hearth, eschewing the lure of the workplace in order to be a constant presence in my children's lives. When I had left my job to have my first baby, no office boasted a computer system. Now, they all did. How was I going to support my family?

"Displaced homemaker" was the term they used for me and thousands of other women like me.

I sat in agency after agency, scribbling applications for training courses and emergency relief. I was assured that help would soon be on the way. But in the meantime, there were bills to pay and five young and hungry mouths to feed. How would I get by?

I babysat a little; I tried telemarketing at night. But until I was accepted into a training program and acquired real skills, every month would prove a tremendous challenge.

One day I couldn't take it anymore. The strain and burden were too great to bear. The next month's rent was due the following day, and I was $240 short. The refrigerator and cupboards were bare; I didn't know what I would serve my children for supper that night. Each month I had somehow managed to pay the rent and feed the kids. But now I seemed at the end of my rope. Everything was unraveling—including me.

I began to weep. I felt utterly alone and helpless. To whom could I turn?

Pray! a voice inside of me urged.

Pray? another voice scoffed.

Why not? I shrugged. It certainly couldn't hurt. Out of the depths of my being, I prayed. From my torment and anguish and heartache and pain, I prayed. I prayed as I had never prayed before.

"Dear God," I prayed, "please help me pay this month's rent and feed my children tonight. I'm not asking you to give me luxuries or extravagance. I'm begging you to allow me to *survive.*"

Just then, there was a knock at the door, and my aunt and uncle burst into the room bearing bags of groceries. I stared at them in shock.

I was taken by surprise not merely because my aunt and uncle lived in a different part of town, but because for years, they had been somewhat estranged from our family and had kept in touch only sporadically. I had not spoken to either of them in months.

Yet here they were, only seconds after I had completed my prayers—flesh-and-blood answers to my supplications!

So frightened was I by the juxtaposition of their sudden and unexpected arrival that I could only stammer my surprise and gratitude.

After they left, I pondered—with awe and fear—the mystery of their auspicious visit. I had not spoken to anyone recently who was in contact with them, and I had been too proud to tell my friends and relatives the extent of my troubles. No one had known that my cupboards were empty.

When I had attempted to ask my aunt and uncle what had brought them to my home, they had casually answered, "Oh, we were just in the neighborhood and thought you could use some extra stuff."

An unsatisfactory answer, indeed.

I was overwhelmed with relief knowing that my children would eat heartily that night. But what to do about the rent?

As I began to unpack the groceries, I noticed a white envelope discreetly tucked into one of the bags. It had my name on it.

I tore it open and found inside twelve crisp $20 bills. $240.

Two hundred and forty dollars is a strange amount of money to give as a gift.

But it was precisely the amount I needed for the rent.

~Anonymous, as told to Yitta Halberstam

THE FUNERAL

In 1984, Gertrude Levine of Queens, New York, received a phone call from the administrator of an older adults' summer camp where, she thought, her mother was safely ensconced.

"Mrs. Levine," the administrator said in a subdued voice, "I am terribly sorry to have to tell you the tragic news, but your mother, Sarah Stern,* just had a heart attack and died in the hospital. I'm so sorry—please accept my deepest condolences."

The telephone slipping from her hand, Gertrude slumped in her chair, dazed and stricken. It was incomprehensible . . . her beloved mother, dead. Especially since she had been so robust and alive, high-spirited and feisty. In contemplating her mother's advancing age, she had often reassured herself that Sarah Stern would give the Angel of Death a run for his money!

"Mrs. Levine, Mrs. Levine," came the administrator's faint voice from the telephone receiver on the floor. "Are you still there?"

Gertrude retrieved the phone from the floor in slow motion, still muddled and disoriented. "Y-yes, I'm here," she responded numbly.

"Mrs. Levine, I feel terrible to throw this at you so suddenly, but someone has to come identify the body."

"I don't think I can bear to do it; I will send a close relative instead."

*The name Sarah Stern is a pseudonym.

"That will be fine Mrs. Levine. And again, please accept our deepest condolences. She loved you so much. Your mother was a very fine woman. She loved you so much. She talked about you all the time, always telling everyone what a marvelous daughter she had."

Gertrude bowed her head in sorrow. She was shattered by the loss of her cherished mother. At the funeral and later, during the first hours of the shiva (the Jewish seven-day period of mourning during which friends and relatives pay condolence calls), her tears flowed unrestrainedly. She told the family members who sat on the low mourning stools with her that the shock was too much for her to absorb.

Several hours after the shiva had begun, the phone rang, and someone handed Gertrude the receiver.

A crisp operator's voice announced, "Collect phone call for Gertrude Levine from Sarah Stern. Will you accept the charges?"

"Collect phone call from *whom?*" Gertrude asked, befuddled.

"Sarah Stern," the operator repeated.

"Is this someone's sick idea of a joke?" Gertrude shouted. "I just buried her!"

"Gertrude!" A beloved and very real voice suddenly came over the line, fretting. "I can't seem to adjust my medicine . . ."

It was her mother, Sarah Stern.

There had been *two* Sarah Sterns at the camp, and the wrong family had been notified! The relative sent to identify the body had been sickened by the sight of a corpse and had given it only a quick, perfunctory look.

"Yeah, sure it's Sarah Stern," she had muttered hastily, eager to depart.

Because coffins are always kept closed during Jewish funerals, and Jewish law prevents viewing of the body, the mistake was never uncovered. Consequently, a stranger was now lying in the family plot!

"You cannot imagine the emotional trauma," sighs Gertrude in rueful recollection as she recounts the saga. "Thinking of my mother dead . . . all the pain and suffering . . . the stress of the funeral and the burial and the commencement of the shiva that followed. I won't even talk about the expense or public embarrassment. But of course all of this faded into insignificance when I considered that my mother was very much alive."

But the story doesn't end here. When Gertrude called the children of the other Sarah Stern to offer her condolences and ask that the family make arrangements to transfer their mother's body out of her mother's burial plot, they were unwilling.

"She's there already," they said, "let her be! Why should we go to all the bother of digging her up, buying a burial plot, and giving her another funeral? Once is enough."

Gertrude was aghast at the suggestion. How could she allow a complete stranger to remain in her mother's burial plot, lying next to her deceased father? She begged the other family to remove their mother's body, but her appeals fell on deaf ears. She had community leaders call on her behalf, but they remained intractable. Finally, with no other recourse left, Gertrude had a local rabbi call the family and tell them he would be forced to obtain a court order if they would not comply. It was this approach that finally worked.

"So are you going to give your mother her own funeral now?" Gertrude asked the family when arrangements had been made. To her dismay, they replied that a gravesite funeral would be sufficient.

"In that case I'm coming!" Gertrude said passionately, having become drawn into the drama of the late Mrs. Stern's life and feeling fiercely protective of her honor.

Besides the immediate family, she was the only one there.

Watching the pitiful proceedings unfold at the stark and lonely graveside funeral, Gertrude felt engulfed by an overwhelming sorrow for the life and death of the second Mrs. Stern. At the same time, she also experienced an epiphany, one that illuminated God's plan.

"I always wondered how and why the bizarre mix-up with my mother occurred," she reflects. "At the sparsely attended funeral, which wrenched my heart, I suddenly understood the larger picture."

"You know," she said to the Stern children after the funeral, "your mother must have really been a very special woman or, at least once in her lifetime, done something extraordinary. Because three hundred people came to her funeral—thinking she was my mother—and paid her homage. Look at what kind of funeral she had today, and think about what kind of funeral she had as a result of that strange coincidence. God wanted her to have an honorable funeral, one that she obviously would never have been accorded otherwise, so He arranged for the coincidence to occur."

Six months later, Gertrude's own mother—the first Sarah Stern—died. Once again, she was given a beautiful funeral, but this time only a hundred people came.

Why the stunning decline in numbers?

"People were tired of going to her funeral!" sighed Gertrude Levine.

~ *Gertrude Levine, as told to the authors*

THE OPEN HEART

*I*f ever there seemed a woman destined for motherhood, it was Annie.* From the time that she had been a toddler, she had always reached lovingly for those younger and smaller than herself. She would squeal in delight whenever one of her mother's friends came visiting with babies, her warm brown eyes crinkling up in happy smiles as she gently planted ardent kisses on the infants' foreheads. And she always offered to "babysit," even though she was barely out of diapers herself.

Despite Annie's own tender age, somehow her mother's friends trusted her from the start. Squalling infants calmed down the moment they were placed in her arms and began cooing contentedly.

"That little girl sure has a knack," the adults would comment as they watched her, awestruck. "She has 'mom' stamped all over her."

Even her name seemed to be a harbinger of the future that awaited her. The name "Annie" was somehow redolent of the fragrant smell of freshly baked cookies, old-fashioned aprons dusted with flour, steaming cups of hot cocoa on lazy Saturday mornings.

"Wait till she gets married," the adults who watched her promised one another with absolute certitude. "She'll have a brood of kids."

* The names in this story are pseudonyms.

Alas, it was not meant to be. Annie got married young enough—just nineteen—and true to the predictions made about her long ago, wanted nothing more than the white picket fence and a minivan crammed with children. Her young husband, Cliff, had a responsible job and was happy to start a family right away. Annie's parents, in-laws, friends, and neighbors waited for the young couple to announce the good news almost as soon as they were married. Fate, however, had decreed otherwise.

"I had a miscarriage," Annie whispered over the phone to her best friend, Leslie, who lived 3,000 miles away.

"You'll get pregnant again real soon, I'm sure," Leslie promised. She had been on the verge of confiding a secret to Annie—the reason for her call—but Annie had blurted out her own news first. Sensitive to her friend's misery, she knew this clearly was not the right time. She would have to tell her eventually, but she certainly couldn't now. How could any decent human being—at the height of her best friend's despair about the loss of a first baby—tell her that she was expecting her own?

Annie and Leslie had been best friends for over ten years and had shared everything in their lives. They had been all of nine when they first met and had grown up together, experiencing life's milestones at practically the same time. They had gotten their first periods, first training bras, and first kisses almost simultaneously, and it was exciting for them to undergo these female adventures together.

As naive youngsters who thought they could write life's scripts, they plotted their futures together. We'll get married to brothers, live in the same house, and be pregnant and have our babies at the same time! they hoped. Of course, real life rarely accords with fantasy, and ultimately, they had married men who were strangers to one another, and they had moved to opposite coasts. And it also appeared that Leslie was going to have the first baby . . . alone.

"It's actually a good sign that you had a miscarriage," Leslie said over the phone with a catch in her voice. "Doctors always say that. It means you're fertile; it means you can have children."

But over the years, Leslie was proven wrong. Leslie kept on getting pregnant, Annie kept on having miscarriages. Annie and Cliff spared no expense in trying to conceive: they traveled all over the world to consult with fertility specialists who might offer them a new treatment or glimmer of hope. But none did.

Leslie began feeling guilty each time she became pregnant again and hid her news from Annie for as long as she could. Instead of the symmetries and synchronicities they had experienced when they were young, the best friends' trajectories couldn't have been more different.

"Another miscarriage," Annie would whisper over and over again to Leslie as the years flew by.

"Another pregnancy," Leslie would restrain herself from announcing, waiting to tell her friend until what seemed like the propitious time. However there never really was a propitious time. If there was anything they did in sync, it was Leslie's pregnancies and Annie's miscarriages. Leslie knew that Annie was happy for her, but still, Annie was human, wasn't she? She had to feel the slightest twinge, if not much more didn't she?

Leslie ached for her friend. She wished that she had the power to give her what she wanted more than anything in the world: children.

People finally began to suggest to Annie that she adopt, but she said she just couldn't. She wanted her own, she told them. She was going to keep trying and never give up. Meanwhile, she took a job at the local nursery school, where she parlayed her love for children into a successful teaching career.

Leslie had seven pregnancies that bore fruit. Annie had seven that didn't. How far their plans—and fates—had diverged!

But everything—even Annie's heartbreaking infertility— dimmed to insignificance when Leslie called the next time with her news.

"Breast cancer," she said with a tremor. "The doctor says it's pretty advanced."

"I'll be there tomorrow," Annie said.

Annie took a leave of absence from her job and flew to California to be with her friend. Leslie's husband, Joey, had his hands full caring for seven kids—ranging in age from six months to fourteen years—and accompanying Leslie to her radiation treatments. Annie took over running the household, and in a perverse twist of fate, finally saw the dreams of her childhood realized. She was ferrying carloads of jostling kids back and forth to school, lessons, and appointments; baking mouth-watering delicacies for hungry young mouths; singing nursery rhymes and telling stories at bedtime. Yet underneath her cheery demeanor was a terrible ache. Please get better, she begged inside. We need you and love you so much.

But the radiation did not help, and the next, last, desperate step in treatment was a bone marrow transplant. Leslie flew to Denver with Joey, leaving her kids in the care of her best friend.

"See ya soon," Leslie promised to Annie and the kids before she left for the airport.

But tragically it would be the last time they were all together.

Leslie died in Denver, and when she did, a part of Joey—her devoted husband of fifteen years—died with her. Almost immediately after Leslie's death, Joey became disoriented and irrational; his eyes glazed over and his sentences were muddled and disjointed. The doctors gave him medication and put him under observation, but his progress was dismal.

"He will have to be institutionalized," they told Annie. He would not be coming back home to California for a long time, they said.

Leslie's parents and in-laws were deceased. Neither Leslie nor her husband had siblings. "What's going to happen to the kids?" Annie asked.

In New York, Annie's husband, Cliff, had begun losing patience. His wife had been gone for over five months, and as much as he had compassion for Leslie and her family, he wanted his wife back.

"You have been an amazing devoted friend to Leslie," he told his wife, "and what you have done for her and her family has been incredible, but it is time to come home."

"Honey, you've been incredible," she told her husband, "and I know I am asking a lot, but I just cannot abandon them like this."

"Well, talk to their lawyer, or whoever is in charge, and make arrangements. I want you home, Annie!"

On the phone, Annie frantically conferred with doctors in Denver. "What is Joey's condition?" she asked. "Is he getting any better?"

"Actually," the doctors replied with regret, "there seems to be a downward spiral here. He is getting worse."

One day, two professionally dressed women in suits rang Leslie's doorbell and asked to see Annie and the children. They were from an agency, they said, that had been mandated by the state to place Leslie's kids in foster homes until such time as their father was psychologically capable of taking care of them himself.

"You mean foster home, don't you?" Annie asked with a quaver in her voice. "You said foster homes. You are going to put them into one home, aren't you?"

The woman blinked at her naive assumption.

"Oh no," one of them said. "That's impossible. Where would we find one family to take seven children? We are going to place each one in a different home."

"But they're siblings," Annie protested. "They're each other's family. They're all they've got now. You can't separate them!"

"Really," one of the women exclaimed in disbelief. "Now where exactly would we find one home that would be willing to take in seven children?"

Annie called her husband that night. "Cliff? There is something we have to discuss."

Annie and Cliff opened their hearts and home to Leslie's kids and officially became their foster parents. Later, when it became apparent that Joey would never fully recover from his illness, they formally adopted all seven. They raised all of them lovingly, and strangers, unfamiliar with the story, never had cause to suspect that they were not Annie and Cliff's biological children.

Today, Leslie's kids are all married and have children of their own. And these children call Cliff and Annie "Gramps" and "Grandma," as they are the only ones they have ever known. And Annie wears old-fashioned aprons coated with flour, bakes homemade cookies, and prepares steaming cups of hot cocoa for her grandkids, who jostle each other in her worn minivan. All of her children live nearby, and Annie gets to see her grandchildren almost every day.

In so many of their young faces, she sees traces of Leslie, and they are poignant reminders of her special friend.

"I wish I had the power to give you children," Leslie had once said.

If only it hadn't been this way, Annie often thought, but in a way . . . you did.

~ *Yitta Halberstam*

THE PROVIDENTIAL POSTER

*I*n 1987, Sister Barbara Cox, a member of the Dominican Sisters of Springfield, Illinois, was cleaning the convent's pantry when she came across a placard lying upside down under the shelf paper.

Hmm, that's strange, she thought, as she tugged at the poster wedged deep inside the shelf. What could this be?

It turned out to be a poster demonstrating the Heimlich maneuver—the kind of poster that one ordinarily finds hanging in restaurants and coffee shops, places where vulnerable patrons are in danger of choking on food.

How did this get here? she wondered. It looks old and musty. . . . Wonder how long it's been here? Well, it's not doing anyone any good lying under the shelf paper, Sister Barbara mused. Might as well hang it up myself, she decided. But where?

The outside of the pantry door didn't seem appropriate. It was too public a place. After all, we're a convent, not a restaurant, she reasoned. I'll just hang it up inside the door, in case we ever need it.

She affixed it to the inside of the door and then closed the door. She meant to tell the other sisters about her discovery of the poster and about what she had done with it, but she had many other things on her mind that day, and she simply forgot. Consequently, nobody else in the convent knew about the poster's existence.

The next day, Sister Barbara was eating lunch with the other nuns in the convent and talking rather quickly and animatedly. Suddenly, she started choking on a piece of food, and, embarrassed, she fled to the kitchen to clear her throat. But as much as she tried, she couldn't drive the morsel of food out of her windpipe where it had stubbornly lodged.

She thought she could clear her throat and expel the food on her own, but with a sinking feeling, she realized that her situation was far more serious than she had first imagined. She couldn't seem to breathe, and when she tried to call out to the sisters in the dining room, she wasn't able to vocalize. She couldn't talk at all.

No air was going in or out of her windpipe, and she was feeling lightheaded and faint. Panic-stricken, Sister Barbara signaled to the other sisters that she needed help. They rushed into the kitchen but looked at her helplessly. None of them were trained in first-aid techniques, and none had ever treated a choking emergency. They didn't know what to do or how to assist her. It was then that she remembered the poster that she had pasted inside the pantry door.

She pointed frantically at the closed pantry door. No one understood why. She continued to gesticulate toward the door, until finally one of the sisters opened it. There they saw the poster demonstrating the Heimlich maneuver and understood that it could save her life.

Sister Clara, one of the tiniest sisters in the convent—all of five feet to Sister Barbara's five feet six—read the instructions aloud while following them in a concentrated and deliberate manner, one at a time, step by step. She did exactly as the poster advised, and though it was her first time performing the Heimlich maneuver, she was successful. A piece of food came flying out of Sister Barbara's mouth, and the emergency was over.

"There's no question in my mind that this was providential," reflects Sister Barbara. "The timing was impeccable. I just happened upon the poster the previous day, and the very next day I was its beneficiary!"

~ *Judith Leventhal*

AN ANGELIC LOVE

A cry in the night from my two-year-old daughter jolted me awake for the third night in a row. As I entered her room, Marissa was sitting on her bed, holding her head and crying. Between sobs, she repeatedly told me that her head was "ouchie."

I was beginning to doubt the assumption I had made several days earlier. Life in our house had been hectic. I had recently opened my own business and was busy preparing for a new baby to arrive in six weeks. Our two girls were also adapting to having a sitter all day while Mommy was working. It was enough to make a thirty-year-old feel like crying and holding her head, too. I had naturally assumed that Marissa was just craving a little attention. Now, however, I was worried.

The next morning and throughout the day, Marissa continued to complain about her head. Her medical checkup was the next day, but I decided that I would call the doctor to discuss my concern. The nurse suggested that if the headaches continued, I should mention them to the doctor during Marissa's checkup.

On February 6, 1997, I explained the situation to the doctor. As I watched him proceed with his examination, I became concerned as he performed simple reflex tests on Marissa's toes not once or twice but several times. He also seemed to spend a great deal of time shining a light in her eyes. A few minutes later, I sat and listened. The doctor explained that headaches in two-year-olds were not very common. Given this fact, coupled with some poor reflex response during Marissa's exam, he wanted to do some tests to rule out anything more serious— including a brain tumor. Just being cautious, he assured me. The MRI procedure that he was requesting would essentially allow the doctors a peek inside her brain. "Brain tumors in children are very rare," he repeated.

After arriving home and calling my husband, David, I immediately called Marissa's grandma, Barb. "Stepmother" never seemed to convey the warmth of the special relationship that Barb and I shared. I was only fourteen when my mother passed away. Looking back, I am impressed at how my father raised three teenage girls alone through the next six years. Although I still longed for my mother, I was a little unsure when my dad remarried in 1987. We'd have to share him with Barb and her two children.

But over the years I discovered a special kind of relationship with Barb. I now had a special mom to do things with; to help plan my wedding, to rush to the hospital when I gave birth, and to love my children as her own grandchildren. I had someone I could talk to about my own mother, someone to share special occasions, and someone to watch over my father. During this difficult time with Marissa, Barb did much to encourage and support me, even though she was dealing with her own bad headache from a sinus infection.

The next week, the strain of waiting for the MRI appointment, fear of the unknown, the daily stress of caring for two little ones, coupled with the raging hormones of pregnancy caused me to crumple one afternoon. I found myself sobbing on the phone to Barb. She, of course, rushed to my house and sat with me and helped to pass the time. She spent some time rocking Marissa and reading to both girls. As the girls napped, Barb told me how hard she had been praying that everything would be fine. The possibility of a brain tumor was unthinkable to her. Marissa had not yet lived, Barb said. Then Barb told me she had prayed that if someone were to have a brain tumor, it should be her, not Marissa. She had lived a life full of love, marriage, children, and grandchildren.

On February 20, my father and Barb sat together in the waiting room at the hospital as the staff began to prepare Marissa for her MRI. She was difficult to put to sleep, but finally, with an IV, she was asleep, and the procedure began. David stayed in the room with her, but because of my pregnancy, I stayed in the waiting room, where Dad and Barb continued to assure me that things would be fine.

The next morning our doctor telephoned with the results. I could hear his relief when he told me that the MRI did not show a brain tumor or anything else serious. The MRI did, however, show that Marissa had a severe sinus infection. At her age that would account for the headaches and perhaps for the coordination problems. The good news was that with three weeks of dosing with antibiotics, the headaches would disappear.

Life in our home seemed to return to normal as we prepared for the arrival of our third child in March. As usual, Dad and

Barb met us at the hospital for the birth of our son, Thomas. After that, I thought things would finally settle down.

Our annual Easter gathering and Easter egg hunt was held at Dad and Barb's house. Barb was very carefree, but Dad seemed very tense. Something just did not seem right. The whole atmosphere that day was very stressful. Almost immediately after my sisters and I returned to our own homes, we phoned one another to try to figure out what was so terribly wrong. We all agreed that Barb and Dad were both acting strange. The following Monday, Dad asked if we had noticed anything different about Barb. She was not acting normally. It started with little things, like randomly changing the channel on the television, but included more serious incidents like shopping excessively. She was also complaining of a constant throbbing sinus headache.

Their family physician dismissed it all as some sort of depression and prescribed an antidepressant, but the next week things escalated. The odd little behaviors became more bizarre. Dad took her to the doctor who was treating her diabetes rather than returning to the family physician. The doctor immediately sent her to the hospital for further testing.

I remember sitting with Barb at the hospital as the neurologist gave her a short, simple test. What day was it? What hospital was she in? What floor was she on? Why was she here? Could she remember the following items: cat, book, chair? Somehow I found the strength not to cry in front of Barb when I saw that she couldn't pass the test. I knew in my heart that something was terribly wrong. Like a child, I suddenly wanted to run away to the playground for a place to hide and cry, as I had done almost sixteen years earlier when my mother had died.

The next day, after an MRI, the doctors made the diagnosis. Barb had a massive brain tumor. The doctors figured that it might have started growing sometime in January when her "sinus headaches" began. By now, it was very large and would require surgery at the minimum. But Barb did not make it to surgery, because the tumor hemorrhaged. My special mom, Barbara Vork Barth, died on April 12, 1997, less than one week after being diagnosed with a brain tumor.

Were the similarities in condition and timing between Barb and Marissa a mere coincidence? Or are there a handful of souls on earth so angelic that they would literally give up their life for someone they love? I believe my heart knows the miracle in our story, but in either case I am grateful for the rare opportunity to have been loved so deeply by two mothers and to have witnessed their courage and commitment to their families.

Although our girls were only four and two when their grandma died, their love for her was strong. The headaches in the night no longer wake Marissa and no longer frighten me. My new challenge is to remember the example of strength and love as I wipe away my daughters' tears and comfort them as they cry for their grandma.

~ *Jill E. Reed*

ACKNOWLEDGMENTS

Yitta and Judith want to thank . . .
Our phenomenal agent, Carol Mann, and our editor extraordinaire, Barbara Berger, at Sterling Publishing, for bringing this project to fruition with savvy, patience, grace, and a great deal of smarts. Also at Sterling, we thank Yeon Kim for the beautiful interior design, David Ter-Avanesyan for the gorgeous cover, Josh Redlich in publicity for his amazing professionalism and great creative thinking, and production editor Lindsey Adams and designer Gavin Motnyk.

Yitta would like to thank . . .
Rabbi Joseph and Devorah Telushkin, veritable icons who truly walk their talk, for all their encouragement, kindness, and amazing desire to help me always. Ginny Duffy and Bill Cunningham, who do the same, with amazing goodwill and indomitable "can do" spirits.

Elie Wiesel, my hero and my late father's friend, who has always bestowed me with great kindness.

Liza Wiemer, an extremely talented writer in her own right, is a devoted friend, a wellspring of love and support. Her encouragement, optimism, and advice are boundless.

If any two people epitomize benevolence, it is Steve Eisenberg and Zeldy Lustig. Their most common responses to any questions are "Yes" or "Of course." This is also true for Rabbi Meir Fund, spiritual leader of Congregation Sheves Achim in Brooklyn. May the world be populated with more people like them.

Raizy Steg and Pesi Dinnerstein are the most incredible friends and pillars of support, love, encouragement, and help that anyone could ever ask for. I am blessed to have them in my life. They are spectacular human beings, and they are God's gifts to me. Although my relationship with Azriela Jaffe has been mainly via e-mail, she is a constant source of guidance, support, and love in my life. Many thanks also to Etta Ansel, Nechama Schreibman, Chaya Sora Sokol, Chanie Reicher, Nechama Rubin, Miriam Maney, and Bella Friedman for being in my life. A great plus of working on the Small Miracles series has been my developing friendship with Judith Leventhal, a zany Lucy to my more sedate Ethel. Our husbands are still scratching their heads, but somehow it works.

My wonderful colleagues at *AMI* magazine, for their constant kindnesses and their tolerance and understanding of my absences during my work on this book. Special shout-outs to Chaya Laya Moskowitz, Malky Weinberger, and Esty Cinner for always being so helpful in myriad ways. Basha Majerczyk may be one of the most brilliant women I know, and it is an enormous pleasure and privilege to work with her and have her make my prose sing. Rechy Frankfurter, senior editor of *AMI* magazine, constantly leaves me with my mouth agape. How does she know everything?

My sister, Miriam Halberstam, a brilliant writer who makes me humble, has been one of my biggest cheerleaders. She constantly encourages me and takes pride in the success of Small Miracles as if it were her own. (She also deviously rearranges books in various bookstores to make sure that Small Miracles titles always end up on the front table!)

My brother, Moishe Halberstam, and his wife, Evelyn, for their love and encouragement, and their children, Chaya and Eli, for giving me such pure, unbridled joy.

My mother-in-law, Sima Mandelbaum, for her devoted, ongoing support, as well as my brothers-in-law and sisters-in-law Chaim and Baila Mandelbaum, and Chaya and Yeruchem Winkler. My most amazing and wonderful children, Yossi and Hena Mandelbaum and Eli and Channa Mandelbaum. Yossi, who is technologically savvy, has tried to "plug" previous Small Miracles books in a host of creative and unusual ways, and has even been kicked off a few websites for mentioning Small Miracles once too often. When Eli was a mere child, on his own (I had absolutely no idea he was doing this) he posted a review of Small Miracles online, saying his name was Dr. Freud Popo. (Popo, really?) His quaint choice of pseudonym should have instantly foreshadowed his eventual choice of career—psychology. And no one could ask for nicer daughters-in-law who are helpful and loving in so many ways.

My father, Rabbi Laizer Halberstam, who invested so much in me and taught me everything I know, and my mother, Claire Halberstam, who loved me more than I ever knew.

My rabbi and inspiration, Shlomo Carlebach, who always brought Heaven down to earth, love to people, and people to life, and served as the compelling impetus for my first book, Holy Brother.

Finally, *acharon acharon haviv* (the last place is reserved for the most beloved), my dear husband, Motty, who has always thrown his full support behind my endeavors, even when they were off the beaten track and may have raised a few eyebrows. His brilliance, uniqueness, extraordinary kindness, and love of all humanity have permeated my life with great richness. He is my ultimate teacher and the wings on which I fly.

Judith would like to . . .

. . . give a special thanks to Yitta Halberstam. Many times, partnerships begin on solid ground, and then, somewhere along the way, issues arise and the ground gives way. In the case of our partnership, the more I know Yitta, the more I have the privilege of watching her work, the more I see how she gives selflessly to those in need, the more I am in awe of her. We have written a best-selling book, but that blessing pales in comparison to the blessing of having Yitta in my life.

I would like to thank Pesi Dinnerstein, who has been my guiding light. Just like a lighthouse that does not sway regardless of the waves that brush up against it, so too Pesi. No matter what the tides may bring, her valiant support is something that I have come to rely upon.

Ashira Edelman is someone who is always striving to grow. Her insights and wisdom continue to help nurture me, and she is an inspiration to all who are lucky enough to know her and work with her.

Aviva Feldman has a unique way of seeing things and it is her steadfast commitment to leading a life of integrity that has made her a great sounding board for ideas that are reflected in this book. For this and so much more, I thank her.

Civia Cahan has a humor and an intelligence that adds so much to my life. I thank her for her unrelenting and unconditional support. It is a true gift to have a friendship that spans decades.

I want to thank Leah Gubitz. Sometimes people come into your life and help crack open a window. Sometimes people can help open a door that was jammed. Through sharing her expansive life experiences with me, Leah peeled away the clouds, which allowed me a peek into the Beyond.

Maurice Mendoza, like the Northern Star, has been an ever-present guiding force. She's not just the best. She's the "bestest." Good to know she's got my back.

I want to thank my mother, who has always expected the world of me and demanded that I expect that of myself. Regardless of any achievement I have made, my mother has always clapped for me and then pointed even higher. The sky is not the limit when it comes to her appreciation, admiration, and support for her children. I am blessed to have a mother who has poured so much love into me so that I can take that pitcher and pour that love into my children.

I want to thank my two sisters. My sister Hedy Feiler and her husband, Myer, who together have raised children whom I am proud to call my family: Jack and Huvie, Aviva and Tzvi, Yisroel and Rachelli, David and Mimi, Anschel and Ettala and Hershy. Their children, their effervescent personalities, their songs and dances brighten every family gathering and bring joy to all. My sister Esty and her husband, Jordan, bring so much humor and love into our lives. Regardless of the circumstances, Esty will find a way to make everyone laugh right through it all. A special shout-out to her son, Aron Tzvi, whom we all adore.

And lastly, I want to thank my husband and children: Jules, who has always been my greatest support—I owe him a gratitude that cannot be put into words. And our three daughters who are our three shining stars; Arielle, Shira, and Tehilla. You are all my inspiration. You are my blessing. You are my Miracle.

One last word from Yitta and Judith:
One last thank-you . . . to God. There are many far worthier writers and books out there in the universe who deserve to capture the imagination of the American people. Tens of thousands of new books are cranked out each year, and sometimes, sadly, the best fall through the cracks. We know that the Small Miracles series could just as easily have shared their fate, and that it is only because of your special blessing, God, that it has over two million copies in print. We are cognizant of that fact always and are deeply grateful.

CREDITS

"Forgiveness," 169–73, by Patricia M. Acker, condensed from *The Dying Teach Us How to Live* (Dayton, OH: Greyden Press, 2013)

"The Antique Glass," 33–37, from "Lessons in Emunah," edited by Naomi Klass Mauer. Copyright © March 5, 1995, *The Jewish Press*

Excerpted from other books in the Small Miracles series by Yitta Halberstam and Judith Leventhal:

Originally published in *Small Miracles: Extraordinary Coincidences from Everyday Life* (Holbrook, MA: Adams Media, 1997):

    Anonymous—"Connections," 190–94; "The Message," 195–96
    Ettie Grossman—"Pennies from Heaven," 197–98
    Yitta Halberstam—"The New Position," 65–68; "The New Kid," 75–76; "The Dinette Set," 79–83; "Paid Forward," 105–7; "Bert," 180–85; "The Customer," 186–89; "Lost and Found," 216–17

Originally published in *Small Miracles II: Heartwarming Gifts of Extraordinary Coincidences* (Holbrook, MA: Adams Media, 1998):

    Anonymous, as told to Yitta Halberstam—"Prayers," 227–30
    Yitta Halberstam—"The Tenant," 199–205
    Gertrude Levine, as told to the authors—"The Funeral," 231–35

Originally published in *Small Miracles of Love & Friendship: Remarkable Coincidences of Warmth and Devotion* (Holbrook, MA: Adams Media, 1999):

    Judith Leventhal—"My Editor, My Friend," 218–21
    Peggy Sarlin—"The Dress in the Window," 206–9; "The Prayer," 210–12; "Strangers on a Bus," 213–15

Originally published in *Small Miracles for Families: Extraordinary Coincidences that Reaffirm Our Deepest Ties* (Holbrook, MA: Adams Media, 2003):

Yitta Halberstam—"The Electricians," 222–26; "The Open Heart," 236–42

We are grateful to our contributors and those who shared their stories:

Patricia M. Acker
Devorah Alouf
Sarah Chanowitz
Susan Fahncke
Sara Gopin
Molly Gordy
Suri Granek
Jennifer Greco
Ettie Grossman
Claire Halberstam
Azriela Jaffe
Jamie Kiffel-Alcheh
Carmen Leal-Pock

Gertrude Levine
Marcia Mager
Pat Berra Reul Malone
Lillian Miller
Lorelei Nachin
Esther Raab
Katrina M. Ratz
Jill E. Reed
Peggy Sarlin
Robin L. Silverman
Nanette Thorsen-Snipes
Colleen Ann Traphagen
Jeannie Williams